INTERPRETING NATIONAL HISTORY

How do students' racial identities work with and against teachers' pedagogies to shape their understandings of history and contemporary society? Based on a long-term ethnographic study, *Interpreting National History* examines the startling differences in black and white students' interpretations of U.S. history in classroom and community settings. Interviews with children and teens compare and contrast the historical interpretations students bring with them to the classroom with those they leave with after a year of teacher instruction. Firmly grounded in history and social studies education theory and practice, this powerful book:

- Illuminates how textbooks, pedagogies, and contemporary learning standards are often disconnected from students' cultural identities
- Explores how students and parents interpret history and society in home and community settings
- Successfully analyzes examples of the challenges and possibilities facing teachers of history and social studies
- Provides alternative approaches for those who want to examine their own views toward teaching national history and aspire to engage in more culturally responsive pedagogy.

Terrie Epstein is Associate Professor in the Department of Curriculum and Teaching, Hunter College, and an affiliated faculty member of the Ph.D. Program in Urban Education at the CUNY Graduate Center.

The *Teaching/Learning Social Justice* Series
Edited by Lee Anne Bell,
Barnard College, Columbia University

Critical Race Counterstories along the Chicana/Chicano Educational Pipeline
Tara J. Yosso

Understanding White Privilege: Creating Pathways to Authentic Relationships Across Race
Frances E. Kendall

Elusive Justice: Wrestling with Difference and Educational Equity in Everyday Practice
Thea Renda Abu El-Haj

Revealing the Invisible: Confronting Passive Racism in Teacher Education
Sherry Marx

Telling Stories to Change the World: Global Voices on the Power of Narrative to Build Community and Make Social Justice Claims
Edited by Rickie Solinger, Madeline Fox and Kayhan Irani

Educator Activists: Breaking Past Limits
Edited by Catherine Marshall and Amy L. Anderson

Interpreting National History: Race, Identity, and Pedagogy in Classrooms and Communities
Terrie Epstein

INTERPRETING NATIONAL HISTORY
RACE, IDENTITY, AND PEDAGOGY IN CLASSROOMS AND COMMUNITIES

Terrie Epstein

Routledge
Taylor & Francis Group

NEW YORK AND LONDON

First published 2009
by Routledge
270 Madison Ave, New York, NY 10016

Simultaneously published in the UK
by Routledge
2 Park Square, Milton Park, Abingdon, Oxon OX14 4RN

Routledge is an imprint of the Taylor & Francis Group, an informa business

Typeset in Caslon by
HWA Text and Data Management, London
Printed and bound in the United States of America on acid-free paper by
Edwards Brothers, Inc

Library of Congress Cataloging in Publication Data
Epstein, Terrie.
Interpreting national history : race, identity, and pedagogy in classrooms and communities / Terrie Epstein. – 1st ed.
    p. cm. – (The teaching/learning social justice series)
Includes bibliographical references and index.
1. United States–History–Study and teaching. 2. Education–Social aspects–United States. 3. Race awareness–United States. 4. Group identity–United States. 5. Multicultural education–United States. 6. High school students–United States–Attitudes. 7. High school students–Social networks–United States. I. Title.
E175.8.E58 2008
973.007–dc22   2008011717

ISBN 10: 0-415-96083-5 (hbk)
ISBN 10: 0-415-96084-3 (pbk)
ISBN 10: 0-203-89096-5 (ebk)

ISBN 13: 978-0-415-96083-0 (hbk)
ISBN 13: 978-0-415-96084-7 (pbk)
ISBN 13: 978-0-203-89096-7 (ebk)

This book is dedicated to my mother, Geraldine Epstein

Contents

Series Editor's Introduction

The Teaching/Learning Social Justice Series explores issues of social justice—diversity, equality, democracy, and fairness—in classrooms and communities. "Teaching/learning" connotes the essential connections between theory and practice that books in this series seek to illuminate. Central are the stories and lived experiences of people who strive both to critically analyze and challenge oppressive relationships and institutions, and to imagine and create more just and inclusive alternatives. My hope is that the series will balance critical analysis with images of hope and possibility in ways that are accessible and inspiring to a broad range of educators and activists who believe in the potential for social change through education and who seek stories and examples of practice, as well as honest discussion of the ever-present obstacles to dismantling oppressive ideas and institutions.

In this timely book, Terrie Epstein examines the critical role of racial position in how U.S. history is taught and what young people accept and/or reject as credible in the history their teachers present. We know that white people and people of color often see race and racism in different ways, with whites more likely to highlight a trajectory of forward racial progress and people of color more often seeing the enduring inequalities linked to continuing racial injustices from the past (Bell, 2003; Bonilla-Silva, 2003). Epstein's book shows this is indeed still the case and presents the remedy that might come from teaching U.S. history critically and in a way that is honest about the centrality of racism in the evolution of our country and its institutions.

Based on extensive classroom observations and in-depth interviews with teachers and students, Epstein finds that students bring to the history classroom an interpretive frame, developed in their families and communities, about racial groups, race relations and rights that leads them to reject information that doesn't fit. According to Epstein, white teachers who develop neither a critical perspective on history nor an in-depth understanding of the role race and racism have played in U.S. history tend to teach history from a perspective that generally aligns with the interpretive frame of white students but conflicts with that held by black students. Thus, white students believe their teachers teach "everybody's history" while black students criticize them for teaching only "white history."

What is needed, Epstein argues, is to teach history from a social justice perspective—one that problematizes the mainstream historical narrative, exposing the roots of racism and other forms of injustice and helping students understand the structural and systemic underpinnings of oppression. Teaching history for social justice also draws from the valuable critiques put forward by members of marginalized groups, taking lessons from how oppressed groups resist and challenge racism in their quest for justice. In so doing, students learn to see history through multiple lenses, broaden their own interpretive frames and gain the knowledge and attitudes needed to generate the social will to finally come to terms with and redress the racial system we inherit and perpetuate to our continuing peril as a democracy. Critical race legal theorist Patricia Williams (1997) writes:

> If we could press on to a conversation that takes into account the devastating legacy of slavery that lives on as a social crisis that needs generations more of us working to repair—if we could just get to the enormity of that unhappy acknowledgement, then that alone might be the source of a genuinely revivifying, rather than a false, optimism.

This book contributes to this vital conversation.

Lee Anne Bell
Series Editor for Teaching/Learning Social Justice
Barnard College, Columbia University
March 2008

References

Bell, L.A. (2003) Telling tales: What stories can teach us about racism. *Race and Ethnicity in Education* 6 (1) 8–25.
Bonilla-Silva, E. (2003) *Racism without racists: Color blind racism and the persistence of inequality in the U.S.* Lanham, MD: Rowman & Littlefield.
Williams, P. (1997) *The rooster's egg*. Cambridge, MA: Harvard University Press, p. 24.

Preface

I have been passionate about the teaching and learning of United States history since studying history in college and graduate school in the 1970s and 1980s. When I became a United States history teacher in the early 1980s in an all white suburban high school in Colorado, I wanted to integrate the lessons I learned about people of color, women and other non-elites into the traditional political and diplomatic narratives presented in history textbooks and public school curricular frameworks. I thought it was important to teach young people in public schools about historical actors beyond presidents and policy makers and about historical events beyond political and diplomatic policies. I also taught a course at a local university, where I met an African American high school teacher enrolled in a master's degree program in history. When I began a unit in my eleventh grade classes on slavery and the Civil War, I asked the teacher, Laura Chapin (pseudonym) if she would talk to one of my classes about enslavement. She graciously agreed.

I expected Ms. Chapin to present the type of information that I had learned about in graduate school as part of the new social history of the 1960s and 1970s. Rather than teaching about enslaved African Americans as passive or infantilized victims with little or no culture, the new social historians highlighted the overt and covert ways that enslaved people resisted dehumanization: they created families and social networks, used religion, song, and literacy to speak and spread words of freedom and organized organizations for protest and escape. Ms. Chapin, however, didn't speak to my all white class about African American resilience or resistance. Instead, she described the deliberate and systemic organization of racism that white people and national, state and local governments had put into place. She began by defining slavery as an economic institution based on white people's exploitation of black labor. She then detailed how whites used national, state, and local political and legal systems—as well as social and psychological terror—to maintain white superiority and black oppression. Finally, she discussed slavery in more personal terms: how white men raped black women for profligacy and profit, how they beat black men into obedience or submission and how white men and women used a range of interactions to strip the enslaved of their dignity and African heritage.

When Ms. Chapin completed her talk, my students and I clapped in earnest, for we were impressed by her knowledge and passion. But we were also stunned into silence. As the dismissal bell rang, no one said a word; it must have been the first time that year that students were silent as they left the room. When thinking about the presentation that evening, I felt defensive and guilty. I argued with myself that the intentions of white people—or at least *Northern* white people—could not have been as deliberate and cruel as Ms. Chapin had suggested. Yet there was nothing in her talk that I had not known. I knew that national, state and local laws, policies and practices created and perpetuated enslavement and I knew that Northern as well as Southern whites had created and profited from free black labor. I was aware that white men beat black men and raped black women; as Ms. Chapin had noted, the complexions of contemporary African Americans ranged from light to dark, phenotypes that resulted from coercion rather than choice. Despite my knowledge, however, I still found it hard to believe and accept the totality of the institutionalization of racism and whites' complicity in it. The next day in class, I didn't say a word about Ms. Chapin's presentation and neither did my students. I continued teaching lessons about nineteenth-century sectional compromises and conflicts;

my students and I never made mention of Ms. Chapin or the historical themes she dared to discuss.

Ten years later, another incident about teaching U.S. history in multiracial schools shook my consciousness. This time, I was an Assistant Professor at Boston College and Jerry, one of my student teachers related the following incident in a student teaching seminar. One of the African American high school students in the Catholic high school in which he student taught asked in class why he and other teachers and textbooks never taught about African Americans' contributions to building the nation. When Jerry asked the student to elaborate, the student commented that he learned from "the [African Americans] community" that "we built this country. We built the railroads, ports, roads in the South, yet you never hear about it in school." The white high school students in Jerry's class scoffed at the suggestion that African Americans had built the South—or contributed much of anything to national development—and black and white students in his class argued heatedly about blacks' contributions to nation building. Jerry had never thought or taught about enslaved or free black labor in the way the African American high school student had articulated it; worse he had no idea of how to deal with the racial hostility which emerged in class. When he asked me how he should have handled the conflict, I sat there in silence.

Many years later as a professor who has taught in public and private colleges and universities, I still find that white teachers have difficulty teaching about the nation's history of white racism and black oppression. Although some teachers today may be more knowledgeable and forthcoming about enslavement and other aspects of race relations, many still teach about enslavement and other acts of institutionalized racism as policy aberrations or moral failings, rather than as integral and ongoing aspects of our nation's legacy. By avoiding teaching about racism and other forms of injustice as significant aspects of U.S. history, teachers present an inaccurate and dishonest representation of the nation's development. They also rob young people of the knowledge and abilities necessary to learn from past injustice, connect past to ongoing systems of oppression and employ individual and collective strategies to resist and challenge inequality. In addition, young people who learn about racism from family and community but not from state or official sources like teachers or textbooks learn to distrust historical and political knowledge taught in schools. By avoiding lessons about racism, educators perpetuate the racial divide between many whites' and non-whites' interpretations of U.S. history and society. Avoidance contributes to the nation's sense of racial amnesia and retards the potential of racial reconciliation.

Teaching U.S. History for Social Justice

As a history educator, I am advocating that teachers (and textbooks, policy documents, and teacher educators) teach U.S. history to promote social justice. To do so means that teachers attend to the interrelationships among three core components. The first is the perspective, interpretation or point of view from which they present historical and contemporary issues. Teaching history for social justice involves teaching about the origins and development of racism and other forms of oppression not simply as problems that have been or need to be solved, but as integral and ongoing systems of power relations that characterize societies past and present. The approach explicates how oppressed people and their allies from dominant groups often acted courageously as individuals and strategically as groups—and at times across racial, ethnic, economic or gender divisions—to struggle for freedom and rights. It also involves teaching about the contributions that marginalized groups made to national development throughout the course of history, rather than mainly during black or women's history month. Although everyone talks about this type of inclusion, this and other studies (Wills, 1994; 1996) make clear that there is more lip service than there are lessons about the contributions that people of color and women have made to the nation's past.

A social justice approach to teaching history also entails teachers taking into account how children's or adolescents' identities influence their views of history, society, and state-sanctioned or dominant historical interpretations presented in schools and the mainstream culture. Nationality, race-ethnicity, gender, religious orientation and other aspects of identity shape and differentiate the interpretive frameworks—the knowledge, beliefs and associations—that individuals bring to historical and social scientific inquiry (Wertsch, 2002). Individuals and communities who identify with dominant groups tend to accept much or all of the knowledge taught in schools and find lessons about the nation's legacy of oppression difficult to accept. Children, adolescents and adults from marginalized communities whose knowledge and experiences have been ignored or discounted in schools have constructed alternative frameworks and distrust or discount historical interpretations which downplay the history of racism and the contributions of non-whites. Teachers who understand the interpretive frameworks through which students construct or critique school knowledge will be better able to create pedagogical strategies which open students' minds to learning about U.S. history from a social justice perspective.

Teachers aware of the ways in which their own national, racial-ethnic, political etc. identities and prior experiences have shaped their views towards history, society, teaching and learning can situate their interpretive frameworks within broader contexts, recognizing the strengths and limitations of their own knowledge and beliefs. This type of self-reflection may make white teachers less guilty or defensive about teaching about racism and white privilege and more receptive to learning from students or adults from marginalized groups. It may also make them more willing to take risks and learn to handle discussions about difficult topics like race relations. To do so involves both opening up oneself to self-reflection and opening up one's classroom by creating safe yet challenging spaces to conduct conversations about oppression and privilege.

These ideas are not just based on my own knowledge and commitments about teaching and learning history in a diverse society. They also are influenced by a growing body of empirical research on the effects of identities on children's, adolescents' and adults' interpretations of history (Epstein, 2006), as well as the findings that emerge from the evidence in this book. The book's major contributions lay in its detailed analyses of how white and black children's and adolescents' racial identities shaped and differentiated students' interpretations of the contributions of racial groups, the consequences of race relations and the course of individual rights in U.S. history and society. These findings are significant because teachers who understand how students' racial identities shape their historical thinking can begin to challenge the limits of students' knowledge and beliefs and do so in ways which might be more effective than those employed by the teachers in the study.

The book also is among the first to address parents' beliefs about the purposes and credibility of school history (Wineburg, Mossborg, Porat & Duncan, 2007) and the role of history in the production of citizenship. It contributes to a very limited literature (Gwaltney, 1993; Rosenzweig & Thelen, 1998; Wineburg, Mossborg, Porat & Duncan, 2007) on adults' uses and/or interpretations of U.S. history and to the effects of race/ethnicity on their views. By interpreting adolescents' uses of history in community settings, the book also is among the first to examine how adolescents engage in and interpret history beyond the classroom door (Dimitriatis, 2000). The findings from these disparate settings and participants demonstrate the breadth and depth of the racial divide in Oakdale, as well as the desire of many within the African American community to disseminate privately and publicly knowledge about their history and experiences. The findings also may stimulate additional research into the under-researched area of historical teaching, learning and performance in family, school and community settings.

Although the work is framed within the literature on teaching and learning history in democratic societies, it also contributes to socio-cultural or diversity studies in education. The book illustrates the significant and specific effects of identity and culture on teaching and learning a specific subject matter in classroom and community settings. But history is more than just an academic subject; it is the reference point—an aspect of identity—from which people derive a sense of themselves, their communities and their place in the world. While much has been written about literacy as greater than reading and writing and tied to people's identities and communities, little comparable work has been done with historical sense making. Researchers and teachers in all fields can profit from understanding how racial, ethnic, gendered, etc. identities shape children's and adolescents' interpretive frameworks on history, society and schooling by promoting pedagogical change which transforms, rather than reproduces, contemporary power relations.

Outline of Chapters

In Chapter 1, I have presented the larger political and cultural contexts which shape the teaching and learning of history and society in and out of schools. The chapter includes a critique of contemporary national and state policies, history textbooks, and history/social studies educational approaches which powerfully influence how many teachers teach about U.S. history and contemporary society. I documented the significant effects that national, racial-ethnic, gender, religious, etc. identities have played in shaping people's interpretations of history and society, the relatively minor effects that classroom pedagogies have played in changing students' interpretive frames and the reasons why teachers find it so difficult to teach about race and conflict. I described the origins and development of the book, as well as the history and a contemporary profile of Oakdale, the community in which the study took place.

In the second chapter, I described how the six white teachers in the study thought and taught about racial groups, race relations, and individual rights in U.S. history and contemporary society. I selected these three broad concepts because these were the ones in which I found significant race-related differences in children and adolescents' interpretations. In addition to categorizing and analyzing teachers' perspectives on racial groups, race relations and individual rights, I include several examples of teachers' actual lessons, as well as students' commentaries, critiques and silences. I also illustrate how the teachers' identities, beliefs and backgrounds affected their interpretations of race and rights in history, as well as their instructional choices.

In the third chapter, I analyzed the effects of children's and adolescents' racial identities and classroom pedagogies on students' interpretations of history. I did this first by analyzing the differences in white and black students' beginning-of-the-year explanations of individual historical actors and events; concepts of the roles of racial groups, the course of race relations, and the expansive or exclusionary nature of rights; and the overarching themes which characterize U.S. history (for eighth and eleventh graders). I then analyzed students' end-of-the-year explanations, concepts and themes and assess what, if anything, changed between the beginning and end of the year (see Appendix C). Because I found similar interpretations within racial groups across the three grade levels, I collapsed the findings from the fifth, eighth and eleventh classrooms into the conceptual categories noted above. I also included adolescents' views about the credibility of school-based historical narratives, which provided further evidence of a racial divide in their interpretations of history, society and the teaching of history in public schools.

The fourth chapter examined the racial divide in white and black parents' explanations and interpretations of U.S. history and contemporary society, as well as in their views about the purposes and credibility of school history. I also described the agency of black adolescents in creating spaces for teaching and learning about African American historical experiences, experiences they believed were marginalized and distorted in history classrooms. Consequently, some black adolescents in Oakdale sponsored or sought out forums to present critical perspectives on black history, critiques of the teaching of black history in schools and the significance of citizenship for black youth and adults. I found very little comparable activity on the part of white adolescents and in the few cases where white youth participated in civic-oriented events, white adolescents presented distinctly different views on the meaning of history and citizenship, views consistent with their positions as members of a racially privileged group whose views were represented in school and the broader culture.

In the final chapter, I discussed the constraints on teachers interested in teaching history for social justice, as well as possibilities that exist for teachers to re-educate themselves about the role of racism and anti-racist struggles in history and today, the ways they can become aware of the effects and particularities of their racial-ethnic identities on their interpretive frameworks, and the means available to learn more about their students' identity-related knowledge and beliefs. Finally, I also presented examples that successful teachers have used to present a social justice oriented approach to history and to open up classroom discussions so that students can talk about race and injustice historically and today in ways which further rather than retard learning about race and history.

Continuity and Change across Time and Place

When I began this project in the 1990s, I imagined that African American students might interpret U.S. history as revisionist historians of the 1960s, 1970s, and 1980s had done and with which I became well versed in college and graduate school. Unlike the history I had learned about in a white working class community in the late 1960s and early 1970s, university professors in the elite universities I attended presented blacks as more than intermittent victims. They taught that enslaved and segregated blacks had created and maintained vibrant black cultures and communities which served as buffers to oppression and means for self-determination. As individuals and community members, blacks used a range of overt and covert means to resist subordination and dehumanization throughout national history, as well as construct multiple and even conflicting perspectives on the means and meaning of black education and/or liberation.

For the most part, however, black (and white) adolescents and adults in the study did not tell stories about black community building, although they did credit blacks collectively with racial progress. Rather, they articulated a much less optimistic perspective on the meaning and significance of black people's historical experiences, even as they expressed respect and admiration for the courage of black historical actors. Rather than focus on black resistance and culture, black adolescents and adults talked about white-on-black violence and exclusion and how blacks dealt with white threats to their physical and mental well being. In short, black participants talked as much about white people's agency in black oppression as they did about black people's subjectivity in racial group or national history. I don't remember this emphasis on white people's agency—as opposed to that of Southerners or slave owners—in my undergraduate or graduate studies.

White participants, on the other hand, discussed white violence towards blacks minimally during enslavement and segregation, and more in relation to Native Americans in the post-Civil War westward movement. They tended to portray blacks as historical subjects only during the Underground Railroad and Civil Rights Movement. I suppose that marks progress: in the racially segregated white working class community in which I grew up, I only remember having learned that Native Americans were exotic and war like, blacks were victimized slaves of Southerners, violence only occurred during wars, and beneficent whites led the Civil Rights Movement. Even in the white dominated elite graduate schools I attended in the late 1970s, the emphasis seemed to be on black agency, culture and resistance, but little on whites' roles in racial oppression, although I don't know if the gap in my knowledge resulted from a failure of the formal education I received, the historical memory I repressed, or the slow pace of change in the teaching of U.S. history in communities like the one I grew up in outside Boston or Oakdale.

Acknowledgments

This book is the product of many years of research and writing and I've had considerable support along the way. The Spencer Foundation provided initial support for my study in one eleventh grade classroom, and generously provided additional grants for data collection in another eleventh grade classroom and two fifth and eighth grade classrooms. During 2007–2008, they have supported my work with another grant, this time to study the effects of culturally responsive teachers (teachers who teach about racism, individual and group agency, etc.) on urban adolescents' historical interpretations and I include in the final chapter some teaching suggestions based on the practices of the two exemplary teachers in New York City public schools that I am observing. Overall, the Spencer Foundation has provided $175,000 for this project and has enabled me to collect data on over 100 children and adolescents, 24 parents and eight teachers (including the New York City study). I am grateful for its support and for contributing to educators' efforts to bridge or at least narrow one aspect of the racial divide in learning.

Other institutions and individuals have supported this work. The University of Michigan's Rackham Graduate School provided over $50,000 in funding, and Hunter College and the City University of New York have provided additional monies and course releases. Several individuals have supported my writing as well: Catherine Bernard and Heather Jarrow, my editors at Routledge, patiently taught me how to turn into a book what I originally presented to them as three articles with an introduction and conclusion. Others who have contributed to my thinking and writing over the years include Keith Barton, Jane Bolgatz, Robby Cohen, Melinda Fine, Michele Foster, Diana Hess, David Gerwin, Michele Foster, Joe Moreau, Linda Perkins, Linda Levstik, Simone Schweber, Avner Segall, Peter Seixas, Diana Turk, and Bruce VanSledright. Several doctoral students at the University of Michigan who are now professors or research directors collected and analyzed data and contributed greatly: these include Jamal Cooks, Adrienne Dixson, Edward Fergus, and Damon Williams. Several other undergraduate and master's students transcribed audiotapes and I thank them for their work. Dean David Steiner at Hunter College and Anne Ediger, Chair of the Department of Curriculum and Teaching, supported this effort in countless ways.

A few people stand out for their enduring (and I mean enduring) support. Carolyn Riehl, Anna Neumann and Aaron Pallas have seen and heard me struggle with this work as it, they and I moved from Ann Arbor and East Lansing, Michigan to New York City and I feel lucky to have them on and by my side. Since coming to New York in 1998, Amy Wells and her family have been a great support and loads of fun; Alan Sadovnik, Susan Semel, and Barbara Winslow have become good friends, without whom this task would have been much more difficult. Although residing in California, Arnetha Ball has been alternately a colleague, next door neighbor, sister, mother and/or psychologist and along with her husband Fred, have been there through thick and thin. Isabel Olivera-Morales, my other "adopted sister," has provided not just emotional support over the years but a wonderful annual vacation destination in Boulder, Colorado. Jeremy Price has been an invaluable friend who has sustained me emotionally through the ups and downs of writing this book, and not just during our Friday night cocktail hour/s. Finally, my dog Jack rarely says a word, loves me no matter what and more insistently than my friends, reminds me there's more to life than work.

I've dedicated this book to my mother who, with all of her human frailties which have become all the more frail over the last years, never failed to love me or let it show.

1

WHOSE HISTORY?

The Role of Identity, Pedagogy, and Power in Teaching and Learning U.S. History

Introduction

At the end of the school year in an eleventh grade U.S. history class, a young man named John gave the following narrative about the course of the nation's history:

> Our country was put together by motivated people and people who wanted to change, to better themselves and our country. That's why they left Europe ... they wanted to establish their own way of life. They wanted freedom of religion and speech and didn't want to answer to a king. The Constitution was about freedom and laws and the Bill of Rights gave us rights. Slaves didn't like being slaves so they rebelled; if this hadn't happened then things might still be this way. They didn't want slavery so they changed it.
>
> Women didn't want to be put down because they were women and wanted the right to vote. So they went and made a change. With immigrants, if we didn't have freedom and rights, then when they came to America, the government could have just sent them back. They did a lot for the country, like made us a melting pot. And [Martin Luther] King [Jr.] helps out today. He's a role model for everybody, shows us that everybody is treated equal, it doesn't matter what race or color you are, everybody should get along.

John told a progressive story of U.S. history, one in which people successfully and relatively effortlessly challenged inequality, the government created and expanded freedom and rights, and civil rights leaders brought equality to all. John held an optimistic view of past and contemporary American society, one which associated a national identity with progress, rights and equality, and one with which he identified personally, as exemplified in his use of "we" and "us" when describing national policy or polity.

Another young man in the same class told a different story at the end of the year about the course of national development and the meaning of national identity:

> It started in Europe where royalty oppressed people, so they started their own country. But then they started oppressing people. Like *Animal Farm*, the pigs were being oppressed but when they got into power, they did the same things. They were bringing slaves from Africa to America because they needed people to work on plantations. After the Civil War, slaves were free but they weren't equal. They still had to be under whites and live by a different set of rules.
>
> There's been progress but these things shouldn't have happened in the first place. It's not necessary to have slavery to build a nation ... The whole thing is about struggle; they had to struggle for a war of independence, they had to struggle to become a superpower. In the Civil Rights Movement, we had to fight, be patient for progress to happen. You have to sacrifice to make a better life. Today blacks still struggle for equality.

Like John, Jamal began his story with a people who escaped oppression, but the oppressed soon became oppressors. While some people struggled to create a new and powerful nation, enslaved and free blacks struggled to achieve freedom and rights. While the nation extended freedom and rights to some Americans, it excluded, enslaved and segregated others. Jamal created a much more tempered view of national history and contemporary society than did John. Jamal associated U.S. history and a national identity with limited progress marked by struggle, racism and inequality and affiliated personally with a collective African American identity, rather than—and often in opposition to—a unified national community.

The above quotes provide a window into the differences into one European American and one African American student's interpretations of U.S. history after they had completed a year of history instruction in an urban working class Midwestern community called Oakdale (pseudonym). Although the two teenagers sat side by side in the same classroom reading the same texts, listening to the same teacher, and taking the same tests, they came away from class with very different ideas about the significance of racial groups' contributions and experiences, race relations and individual rights in the nation's history and contemporary society. And John and Jamal were not unique: the differences in their interpretations about race and rights were representative of a majority of the 100 students interviewed for this book. As demonstrated in Chapters 3 and 4, I found a deep and enduring racial divide in how Oakdale's African American (hereafter referred to as "black") and European American ("white") elementary, middle and secondary students represented race and rights in national history and contemporary society, a divide which originated in the distinct linguistic and social practices in which white and black children, adolescents and adults participated.[1]

The racial divide in young people's historical and contemporary interpretations have prompted a number of questions about the role of interpretive differences in teaching history. Was John's and Jamal's teacher, for example, aware of differences in their understandings at the beginning of the year? Did she or how did she manage these differences and what effects did her pedagogy have? What role did the teacher's racial identity play in her pedagogy and how did she deal with the difficult issues surrounding the teaching of racism in history? And what were the possibilities and limitations of her or other teachers' pedagogies in challenging and changing students' understandings, especially as they related to controversial issues like race? In general, what is the potential, for teachers in monocultural or multicultural classrooms who want to teach U.S. history for social justice, i.e. teach in ways that enable students to acknowledge the legacy and ongoing reality of racism while at the same time provide opportunities for students to learn about individual and collective agency to challenge racism and other forms of inequality?

The purpose of this book is to examine the role that classroom pedagogies and racial identities played in shaping the interpretive frameworks—or web of knowledge and beliefs (Wertsch, 2002)—which shaped children's and adolescents' explanations of historical actors and events, as well as their interpretations of the major themes which structure narrative accounts of national history and contemporary society. Based on interviews with and observations of over 100 children and adolescents, two dozen parents and six teachers between 1995 and 2000, I investigated the role that family, teachers, peers and local community activities played in forming and reforming Oakdale's black and white students' understandings of our past and present society, particularly as they related to issues about the role of racial groups, the nature of race relations, and the course of individual rights.

The investigation led me into the classrooms of six teachers (two fifth grade, two eighth grade and two eleventh grade) who volunteered to participate, where a research team of doctoral students and I interviewed 60 students (10 per classroom) and observed countless lessons. We also interviewed 24 of the students' parents to learn about their interpretations of history and contemporary society, the stories about the historical experiences of relatives and historical figures they discussed with their children at home, and their views of the purposes of teaching history in a diverse democratic society. I also observed and/or interviewed 40 adolescents who initiated or participated in a variety of community events related to history and civic society. Each participant and setting provided additional evidence into the different, and in many cases opposing, meanings that black and white children, adolescents and adults constructed about race and rights in national history and contemporary society.

My purpose in writing this book also is to provide a text which improves educational practice by providing examples of the positive and harmful ways in which teachers actually taught about race and rights and including approaches for teaching national history in ways which promote social justice. By this I mean presenting a U.S. history curriculum which acknowledges the significant and enduring role that racism and other forms of inequality have played—and continue to play—in our national history and contemporary society. It also means teaching about the multiple ways that individuals and groups within and across racial lines have struggled to extend freedom and equality and teaching about individual and group agency in ways which students can grasp as models for their lives and times. As one young woman in the study commented in a speech at a luncheon for black youth, "not everyone can be Martin Luther King Jr., but everyone can make a difference and serve the community by standing up for what's right."

Teaching U.S. history for social justice also includes teaching students to critique historical and contemporary texts not just as academic historians do, but as critical minded citizens do, noting whose facts are presented as "what happened" or as "the truth," as well as who benefits and who is silenced by particular interpretations of the past and present (Segall, 1999). Perhaps hardest of all, teaching national history for social justice involves teachers in the difficult business of creating and managing classroom discussions and activities about racial and other forms of privilege and oppression, an enterprise which involves teachers and students in very personal and emotional public engagements (Fine, 1993; Trainor, 2005; Barton & Levstik, 2004). Talking about racism historically and today is difficult, especially in multiracial classrooms or those in which the teacher and students have different identities or interpretive frameworks. But teachers who avoid race talk in history or humanities classrooms mis-educate all American youth not just about their nation's historical legacy, but about their ability to change contemporary society.

This book is the first to document, analyze and interpret race-related differences in children's and adolescents' explanations and interpretations of U.S. history in and beyond classroom settings. It illustrates the profound effect that racial identities played in shaping young people's historical interpretations and contributes to a broader set of studies on the role of culture (i.e. nationality, sub-nationality, race-ethnicity, gender, generation and religion) in shaping historical interpretation (Barton & McNully, 2005; Epstein, 2006). Grounded in socio-cultural theories of learning, cultural studies of historical thinking have contributed to existing cognitive studies. Cognitive studies have examined young people's reasoning about historical epistemology and promoted teaching history in ways which enabled young people to construct and critique historical texts in academically rigorous ways (Seixas, 1993; Shemilt, 1980; VanSledright & Brophy, 1992; Wineburg, 2000). Cognitive studies, however, have not taken into account how culture, broadly defined, shaped young people's historical thinking. Socio-cultural studies have broadened our understanding of how cultural identities like nationality, race-ethnicity or religion influence people's interpretations of the past. They, like the findings in this book, demonstrate that teaching and learning history is much more than a cognitive or academic exercise about argumentation or evidence; teaching and learning are cultural and political acts in which schools promote state sanctioned knowledge and silence alternative interpretations of history and society.

The book is also the first ethnographic study to examine the effects of family/community discourses and classroom pedagogies on children's and adolescents' historical interpretations and on adolescents' interpretations of history and society in community settings. Schweber (2004, 2006; see also Schweber & Irwin, 2003) has written several thoughtful studies on the effects of teachers' and students' cultural identities on their interpretations of the Holocaust, and Dimitriadis (2000) has written about black adolescents' discourses about U.S. history in a community setting. This is the first book-length study, however, to examine the effects of identity and pedagogy within classroom and community settings. As a consequence, it has illuminated teachers' silencing of black students' historical interpretations, the limited effects of teachers' pedagogies on black and white students' historical interpretations and black students' responses to silencing by presenting their views of history and school knowledge in school and community wide settings.

Teachers' silences or marginalization of conversations about race also had adverse effects on white students. As other studies in other settings have documented (Grant, 2003; Trainor, 2005), white students in Oakdale often resented or felt defensive when learning about the victimization of people of color and believed they were being blamed for the nation's legacy of racism, in which they believed they've had no part. Like teachers nationally (Levstik, 2000), teachers in Oakdale sometimes struggled with balancing the nation's legacy of racism with the fear of alienating young people from affiliating with a national identity. Most often, however, the teachers' limited curricular presentations about racism to events like slavery or segregation and avoided conversations about race. The contexts in which Oakdale teachers and teachers nationwide have taught U.S. history have worked against their learning to become better equipped to teach students whose interpretations differ from their own and in ways which promote a more social justice oriented history of the nation.

Contexts for Teaching and Learning U.S. History in Schools

Interpretations of U.S. History in Textbooks and State Standards

U.S. history textbooks and national, state and school district curricular frameworks and learning standards have played and continue to play important roles in determining the interpretations of U.S. history taught in public schools. Since their inception (Moreau, 2003; Zimmerman, 2002) history textbooks have structured national history around the contributions, experiences and interpretations of elite white men, marginalized the contributions and experiences of people of color and women, ignored the violent and oppressive nature of racism, and underemphasized the role that political and social movements have played to challenge government power (Loewen, 1995). They've presented national development as the progressive unfolding of democratic policies, with notable exceptions related to a few incidents in the nation's treatment of people of color; presented people of color sporadically, oftentimes comparing their experiences with those of European immigrants; and minimized and distorted the nation's legacy of violence and oppression of people of color (Banks, 2004; Epstein, 1993; King, 1992; Levstik, 2000; Loewen, 1995; Sleeter & Stillman, 2005; Wynter, 1992). Although textbooks written in the last few years have expanded their coverage of people of color to include both their contributions and their experiences of oppression, as well as presented national policies more critically, they still credit the nation with having done more to dismantle rather than perpetuate inequality and present contemporary society as continuing the nation's legacy of expanding democracy.

State and school district learning standards and curricular frameworks on national history also have presented nationalist views of U.S. history and government. In an analysis of the state of California's history-social sciences curricular framework, Sleeter & Stillman (2005) found that although the framework made reference to diversity and the contributions that people from all races and ethnicities had made to national development, 77 percent of the historical figures included as significant were white (18 percent were African American, 4 percent were Native American, 1 percent Latino and 0 percent Asian American). The framework presented U.S. history as a nation of voluntary immigrants and marginalized the forced migration of Africans to the Americas, the conquest and incorporation of Mexicans in the Southwest and West and the decimation and expropriation of Native Americans. The framework emphasized the nation's founding on a Judeo-Christian heritage and principles of democracy and downplayed the nation's disregard of those principles for most of the population until the twentieth century.

The social studies curricular framework in Michigan, where my study occurred, also emphasized citizens' commitment to democratic values and ignored the nation's lack of commitment to those values (Michigan Department of Education, 1996). According to the framework, the purpose of social studies education was the production of citizens who

> comprehend the ideals of democracy, cherish them, and strive to live their lives in accordance with them. A reasoned commitment to democratic values motivates citizens to safeguard their rights, to fulfill their responsibilities as citizens and to honor the dignity of all people. (p. 34)

The framework, however, did not acknowledge that the nation systematically violated people's rights, enslaved or expropriated people of color, or legally considered women to be second class citizens. Terms such as racism, sexism, or discrimination did not appear. While recognizing the need for students to understand "our commonalities and our diversity exemplified by race, ethnicity, social and economic status, gender, region, politics, and religion" (p. 35), it made no mention of how power and privilege structured and reinforced differences among groups. Like other state social studies frameworks (Apple & Buras, 2006; Cornbleth & Waugh, 1995; Symcox, 2002), Michigan's framework paid lip service to "diversity," but not to historical and contemporary realities of racism and other forms of social injustice.

More recent educational reforms like NCLB requirements around high stakes testing promote teaching and learning about the nation's history as having been founded on principles of democratic rule and individual rights which eventually extended to all Americans (Grant,

2006). The problem with this interpretation is that it does not portray accurately the nation's legacy of exclusion: millions of people for most of our history have been excluded from the "guarantees" of freedom and equality (Keyssar, 2000: Smith, 1997). It also contradicts the knowledge, experiences and beliefs of millions of Americans who have been and continue to be shut out of the American dream by virtue of their race, ethnicity, nationality, sexual orientation, immigration status and the like. As a consequence of teaching a disingenuous national history, millions of young people leave the public schools knowing a nationalistic perspective but not believing it, while those who accept it have no framework for understanding racism and other forms of inequality today. Neither group of young people comes away with lessons of what they might learn from the nation's historical legacy to challenge inequality today.

Teachers' Interpretations and Discussions of U.S. History

Many classroom teachers find it difficult to engage students in discussions about race and the nation's failures to live up to its democratic principles. In one study, Levstik (2000) found that white history teachers identified with whites historically and strongly believed in the progressive improvement in race relations over time. Many considered racism and other forms of inequality as aberrations to the nation's development, and believed that in contemporary society, most injustices have been overcome. Several feared that teaching about race relations or other conflicts might defeat the purpose of teaching history as a way to unify students across racial, ethnic and religious lines. In an earlier study, NcNeill (1986) similarly found that social studies teachers avoided lessons about historical controversies because teaching about conflict made it more difficult to cover the prescribed curriculum and to manage student discussion and behavior. Ironically, both researchers found that middle and high school students thought their history classes would have been more interesting and their teachers more credible if teachers included more content related to conflict and controversy (Levstik, 2000; McNeill, 1986).

Teachers also have resisted discussions of race or racism because they believed it is too complex to discuss with young children, too difficult emotionally for older students and/or too offensive to parents (Bolgatz, 2005; Derman-Sparks & Ramsey, 2006; Lewis, 2003, Sleeter, 2001). Some feared that focusing on the nation's complicity in racism would undermine students' sense of national identity and others believed they lacked the knowledge and skill to discuss racial issues in class (Levstik, 2000). In classrooms where student discussions about race led to heated arguments, teachers often used their authority to shut down discussions rather than risk further discomfort or controversy (Bolgatz, 2005; Fine, 1993; Lewis, 2003; Pollock, 2004). Fine (1993), for example, illustrated how a teacher successfully encouraged students to debate their views, but when students responded angrily to others' comments, the teacher defused the debate by changing the subject. Many history teachers have never received training on handling discussions about race. Few are aware of how young people's racial identities affect their historical interpretations and teachers who venture into the risky territory of race often do so in limited contexts.

Effects of Teachers' Pedagogies on Students' Historical Interpretations

History teachers who have challenged white students' stereotypical views of people of color and discussed white racism have had some limited success in changing students' understandings. As a result of instruction, white elementary school students' explanations of Native Americans in early America changed from exotic and warlike to culturally diverse victims and perpetrators of violence. They also had greater empathy for Native Americans (Brophy, 1999; Wills 1994; Wills, Lintz, & Mehan, 2004). White adolescents who studied slavery learned to see blacks as historical subjects who resisted racism and the students were angered at whites' exploitation of blacks (Wills, 1996; Wills, Lintz, & Mehan, 2004). As the teachers moved beyond the counter-stereotypical lessons and reverted to positive portrayals of powerful whites and national policies, the students reverted to their prior negative stereotypes of people of color (Brophy, 1999; Wills, 1994, 1996; Wills, Lintz, & Mehan, 2004). Although the teachers provided history lessons and units which discussed white racism and positively portrayed people of color, sporadic lessons or units throughout the year were not enough to systematically change students' stereotypical views.

Effects of Racial Identities on Interpretations of History and Contemporary Society

Given that schools and the mainstream media in the United States have privileged the historical contributions, experiences, and perspectives of whites, it is not surprising that many white adolescents and adults have accepted nationalist or state-sanctioned accounts of U.S. history and society. They've considered U.S. history teachers and textbooks as credible sources of information and were more likely to trust school-based historical accounts than eyewitness or family members' accounts (Epstein, 1996, 1998; Rosenzweig & Thelen, 1998). They've identified personally or collectively with the nation's history, situated family experiences within a nationalist interpretive framework, and looked to individuals rather than groups or social movements as models for changing contemporary society (Epstein, 1996, 1998, 2006; Rosenzweig & Thelen, 1998). As a result, white adolescents and adults have been satisfied with the content of the school history curriculum and haven't been voices of change.

African American, Latino and Native American adolescents and adults on the other hand, have developed more critical perspectives on nationalist views of history (Almarza, 2001; Barton & Levstik, 1998; Epstein, 1997, 2000, 2001, 2006; Rosenzweig & Thelen, 1998; Gwaltney, 1993; Terkel, 2005). Black adolescents and adults have placed less credibility in history teachers or textbooks than in eyewitnesses or family members' historical accounts (Epstein, 1998, Rosenzweig & Thelen, 1998), Mexican American adolescents and Native American adults believed that school history ignored their groups' histories (Almarza, 2001; Rosenzweig & Thelen, 1998). Black adults also situated family members' experiences within the context of blacks as a racial group and considered the historical actions of blacks as a collective, rather than as individuals, as a model for changing society (Rosenzweig & Thelen, 1998). Because many history teachers and textbooks presented nationalist interpretations which emphasize the positive role of whites and ignore or distort the roles of people of color, adolescents and adults often have discredited the interpretations of U.S. history taught in public schools.

White adolescents and adults of color also hold different views on racism in contemporary society than do people of color. In national surveys, black adults were more than twice as likely as whites to explain racial income gaps and unequal job opportunities as due to racism. White adults attributed occupational, income and educational disparities to blacks' lack of effort or some other reason related to the role of individual (Kinder & Sanders, 1997; Schuman, Steeh, Bobo, & Krysan, 1997; Sears, Bobo, & Sidanius, 2000). Youth of color also were more critical of contemporary society: adolescents of color were more likely than white youth to consider racism and inequality as major problems in contemporary society and distrust the government to promote more equitable relations (Bell, 2002; Cooks & Epstein, 2000; Niemi & Junn, 2005; Rubin, 2007). Students of color also have had fewer discussions about current events in history or civics classes and few students have had much exposure to discussions about racism or other controversial topics (Niemi & Junn, 1998). Because students of color encounter few opportunities in schools to discuss racism in history or contemporary society, they not just discredit school based accounts but find other avenues to learn about and represent their views.

Overall, national and state educational policies, as well as teachers' pedagogies, have reinforced views of U.S. history and contemporary society as a democratic state which has progressively extended rights to all and racism and other forms of inequality have been overcome. States and the national government promote the interpretation to produce future citizens who will identify positively with the nation and support contemporary policies. At the same time, many white teachers have resisted teaching about racism for fear of provoking anger or losing control in classrooms with students of color or for fear of presenting unpopular or un-American views with which white parents or students might object. Social studies educators and others interested in history teaching have responded with different approaches to educating teachers to teach about the role of racism in history and the differences in young people's explanations and interpretations.

Social Studies Education and Teaching U.S. History

Nationalist Perspectives on Teaching History Educators have proposed distinct yet overlapping approaches for teaching about race and rights in history and contemporary society. As mentioned earlier, learning standards in most states promote a nationalist approach the purpose of which is to instill in the young a commitment to the contemporary nation and civil society (Cornbleth & Waugh, 1995; Grosvenor, 2000; Seixas, 2000; Symcox, 2002; Wertsch, 2002). A "nationalist" approach constructs a direct relationship between the progressive unfolding of political rights and economic opportunity and a positive perspective on contemporary society (Bennett, 2003; Ravitch, 1990; Schlesinger, 1992). Nationalists contend that the racial and cultural diversity of the population has contributed positively to national development and although the nation originally denied people of color, women and others freedom and citizenship rights, disenfranchised groups used democratic principles and practices to struggle for freedom and equality. Gradually the nation extended freedom and equality to all and the accomplishments of disenfranchised groups, as well as the nation's steady unfolding of freedom and rights, illustrated the strength of the nation's democratic creed. Today the gap between the nation's democratic principles and undemocratic practices has narrowed if not completely disappeared, and racism, sexism and other signs of inequality are insignificant compared to the freedoms and rights that Americans share in contemporary society.

Disciplinary Perspectives on Teaching History Disciplinary approaches to teaching and learning history promote cultivating in the young the epistemological orientation and skills of professional historians (Davis, Yeager, & Foster, 2001; Levstik & Barton, 2005; Seixas, 1993, 2000; Shemilt, 1980, 2000; VanSledright, 2002; Wineburg, 2000). Proponents advocate organizing the teaching and learning of history around the acquisition of conceptual categories—historical significance, empathy, causes and consequences—that historians use to structure historical narratives and explain why, as well as how, historical actors, events, or periods acted or unfolded. They also promote the acquisition of procedural knowledge—the analysis and evaluation of primary and secondary sources, the synthesis of sources into historical accounts, etc., that historians employ to critique and construct historical texts. Unlike other approaches, a disciplinary approach to history education does not privilege particular content, themes, or interpretations in teaching history. Rather advocates seek to impart to the young concepts and skills of historical analysis, synthesis and judgment, as well as dispositions like disciplinary distance so that young people will avoid imputing contemporary ways of thinking and behaving to past people and events (Seixas, 2000; Shemilt, 1980, 2000; VanSledright, 2001; Wineburg, 2000).

Participatory democratic perspectives on teaching history Participatory democratic perspectives relate the teaching of history to the promotion of active citizenship in contemporary society. Embodied in the learning standards of the National Council for Social Studies (1994), as well as in the writings of several scholars (Banks, 1997; Barton & Levstik, 2004; Parker, 2003), the approach encourages young people to recognize the multifaceted nature of social issues and draw upon a wide range of knowledge to solve contemporary problems. People of color, women and others contributed to national development but struggled over the centuries and continue to demand freedom and equal rights today. Although the nation established documents with democratic principles, the principles only extended to white males and excluded people of color, women and others from democratic practices. They learn to appreciate the gap between the nation's ideals of equality and realities of inequality and by engaging students in discussions of controversial issues, they learn to reason about their views and learn from students whose views differ from their own (Hess & Posselt, 2002). The perspective promotes the education of citizens who analyze the roots of contemporary problems, argue effectively and respectfully in public settings, promote social equality and act on decisions to promote the common good.

Critical perspectives on teaching history Critical scholars see the teaching of history as a means to enable young people to develop skills to disrupt oppressive hierarchies and work towards a more equitable society (Hursh & Ross, 2000; Ladson-Billings, 2003; Segall, 1999; Stanley, 2001). Racism, sexism, capitalism, globalization, and other oppressive power relations are inherent in the nation's past and present; critical scholars want young people to learn how powerful groups oppressed marginalized people and how marginalized groups resisted and fought against exploitation. The nation's democratic principles masked and continue to make invisible unequal power relations, although the schools and mainstream society blame people of color, immigrants and others for unemployment, violence, and other social problems. By teaching young people to analyze how past and present economic, political, etc. structures have produced racial, ethnic, gendered etc. oppression, as well as how contemporary texts "blame the victim" for national problems, the young become critical citizens who critique historical and contemporary power relations and participate in social movements aimed at a more just society.

Critique

The various approaches to social studies education have different implications for the teaching of history and promotion of citizenship, and the latter two promote the teaching of history for social justice (Barton & Levstik, 2004). Only the participatory democratic perspective, however, focuses on engaging students seriously in listening and talking across differences to learn from and respect other people's knowledge and beliefs. Teachers who recognize how children's and adolescents' racial identities shape their interpretations of history and society will be better equipped to fashion pedagogical interventions which respect the diversity of young people's interpretations and promote classroom discussions which enable young people to learn from their differences (Epstein & Shiller, 2005). Young people who learn from teachers and peers about the historical roots of racial conflict, the nation's role in maintaining or dismantling inequality, and the activities of people who challenged inequality may be better able to comprehend and act on issues of injustice in their own communities and the broader society. To teach U.S. history for social justice, teachers need extended knowledge about race and rights in history, students' identity-related historical and contemporary explanations and interpretations, and skills in fostering discussions about controversial and painful issues, like race relations and exclusion from participation in the American dream.

The Book's Evolution and Description

Initial Studies

In the 1990s, I was an Assistant Professor at the University of Michigan and interested in observing a history teacher who taught about race in

U.S. history. I approached Jane Campbell (pseudonym), a black woman who was chair of Oakdale High School's history department. She recommended that I observe Paula Hines (pseudonym) because she had a good relationship with white and black students, would be receptive to a visitor from the university and had recently received a master's in history at a local university. A white woman in her late forties, Paula Hines had 14 years of teaching experience at Oakdale High School and took master's degree courses on African American and women's history in order to provide some "balance" to the traditional narrative on national history. I observed several lessons in two of Ms. Hines' eleventh grade classes on the Constitution and Bill of Rights, enslavement and Reconstruction, World War II and the Civil Rights Movement. At the end of the school year, I elicited students' views of significant historical actors and events, the credibility of secondary historical sources, and the stories and experiences that family members and others talked about at home (Epstein, 1998).

White and black students in Ms. Hines's class had constructed different views of important historical actors and events in U.S. history and even when they considered the same actor or event to have been important, they gave different reasons for their significance. White students selected George Washington because "he was the first president and helped to create the nation" and John F. Kennedy because he "revived patriotism and cared about ordinary people" like themselves. They also selected Martin Luther King, Jr. because he "had a dream or made a difference." They selected the Civil War for "keeping the nation together and ending slavery," the Constitution/Bill of Rights for "having given us our rights," and the American Revolution and other wars for "making us our own country" and a "world power." Overall, two-thirds of the white students' selections and explanations of significance related to nation building or rights and 20 percent related to black freedom or equality. White students expressed themes about freedom, democracy and rights in their explanations of historical actors and events and rarely referred to racism or limits on rights.

Black students selected a different set of actors and events or gave different explanations for similar selections. They selected Martin Luther King, Jr., Malcolm X and Harriet Tubman for "having a dream about black freedom or rights" or "stopping the fighting between blacks and whites." They selected the Civil Rights Movement as important because "people fought for black rights," as well as the Civil War and slavery and emancipation because they "ended slavery and that's when we became free." Sixty-six percent of the black adolescents' explanations related to black experiences; 25 percent related to nation building or individual rights. Black students highlighted the struggle and attainment of black freedom and rights and white violence towards blacks during slavery and the Civil Rights Movement. Although I hadn't interviewed the students at the beginning of the year, it was obvious that their explanations of historical actors and events, and the themes that typified the national experience, transcended or superseded what they had learned in class.

In interviews with students about the history they had learned about at home, the racial divide in students' and families' experiences and storytelling was profound. White working class family members embedded stories about family experiences within frameworks which were congruent with the historical narratives presented at school. They attributed change over time to economic and social improvement or liberalization ("you have much more today than when I was growing up"), black political progress, and the decline of national values represented by differences in positive attitudes towards World War II ("we fought for democracy") and the Kennedy administration ("he cared for the little people") on the one hand, and negative attitudes towards the Vietnam War ("we wasted a lot of lives") and Nixon's administration ("the guy was a liar and a crook") on the other. The stories that family members told about their past experiences fit neatly into the chronology, content and interpretive context of the historical narratives that students had learned about in school and through the mainstream media.

Black family members also told stories of progress, war and generational shifts, but the stories were set against the backdrop of racism running throughout national history. They attributed progress in the economic and social opportunities that their children faced to the struggles of blacks collectively ("there's still racism, but it's nothing like it was in the 1950s, the South etc."), as well as to people like King, Parks, and Malcolm X who served as moral or political exemplars ("she didn't sit in the front of the bus for you to be running to the back"). The theme of racism also marked family members' discussions of World War II ("they had segregated units back then; whites didn't think we could fight as well as them"), the Vietnam War ("there was a lot of racism even though blacks and whites were fighting side by side") and the first Iraq War ("my uncle didn't go, he said why should he fight for freedom over there when the black man doesn't have freedom right here") highlighted the continuity of racism over time. These stories did not match up well to the historical narratives presented at school and through the mainstream media.

While I thought these differences were significant, I wanted to know more. How did young people interpret "the whole story" of national history and what effect did school instruction have on young people's historical explanations and interpretations? Oakdale schools required U.S. history in the fifth, eighth, and eleventh grades, and I was interested in how students at each grade level interpreted national history before and after a year of instruction. During the late 1990s, several graduate students and I collected beginning- and end-of-the-year data in the classrooms of two fifth grade, two eighth grade and two eleventh grade white teachers who volunteered to participate. In each of these, we interviewed 10 students (5 black and 5 white), for a total of 20 students per grade level, or 60 students overall. We matched students by academic achievement and gender between racial groups; within racial groups, we interviewed high, middle and low achieving students. Black graduate students interviewed black children and adolescents, as well as 12 black parents (6 fifth graders' and 6 eighth graders' parents). I interviewed the white students, teachers and 12 white parents. The graduate students and I also observed several lessons in each classroom on race relations, individual rights, and national policies related to race and rights.

Research Task and Data Collection

To elicit fifth graders' and their parents' explanations of historical actors and events, the graduate students and I asked them to explain 16 historical actors and events depicted on captioned picture cards (Appendix A). Eighth and eleventh graders selected and explained 20 of the most important actors and events from a set of 42 picture cards (Appendix B). The picture cards represented traditional nation building actors and events like George Washington, the American Revolution, and World War II, as well as actors and events related to black history, such as Crispus Attucks, slave rebellions, and blacks in World War II. The students completed the task at the beginning and end of the year and the teachers at each grade level discussed the historical actors and events represented by the cards. We analyzed the data within and between racial groups and at the beginning and end of the year. The former enabled us to compare intra- and inter-group similarities and differences in interpretations, while the latter allowed us to assess the effects of the teachers' pedagogies on students' historical views (see Appendix C for a complete description of the research methods).

The graduate students and I also observed and took field notes on lessons in each classroom and paid particular attention to discourses and texts on Native Americans, African Americans, the role of whites in racial oppression, the American Revolution, the Constitution/ Bill of Rights, and segregation and the Civil Rights Movement, for which I found race-related differences in the earlier study. We also became involved in extra-curricular and community-based activities. We sponsored the high school's Black Student Association (BSA) and participated in annual Kwanzaa celebrations, videotaped the BSA's annual Black History Month assembly, and analyzed copies of the *Amistad*, an underground high school newsletter published by "16 African Americans under the age of 21 who are trying to get up and do something in their community."

I also served as a judge for a community organization's oratory contest for middle school students which attracted equal numbers of white and black participants. I judged the oratory contest for the local NAACP's ACT-SO (Afro-American Cultural, Technical, and Scientific Olympics) competition for high school students and chaperoned Oakdale high school students when they attended the annual "Black History Makers of Tomorrow" luncheon, a McDonald's Corporation event which sponsored a regional essay contest for black students. I found no comparable school-wide or extra curricular activities related to history that the white students participated in and the only civic-related activities that students described having participated in, other than church-related activities, were those of a community organization's oratory contest. A few students noted that they formerly participated in an after-school club at the local airport and learned about the history of aviation. But the club was disbanded in the early 1990s due to lack of membership.

In the following chapters, I focus on race-related differences rather than similarities in students' explanations and interpretations because I'm interested in assisting teachers in providing more equitable approaches to teaching U.S. history, especially in classrooms with diverse student bodies. I believe that teachers can learn to teach history for social justice but only if they are aware of their students' pre-instructional understandings and the kinds of curricula and instruction which reinforce or challenge students' understandings. The findings on students' interpretations in Chapters 3 and 4 provide necessary background knowledge for implementing social justice oriented history instruction. And because most of the teaching examples in Chapters 2 and 3 illustrate ineffective curricular or instructional approaches, they provide important lessons on what didn't work or on how to extend an effective practice throughout the course of a year. In the final chapter, I acknowledge both the constraints on teachers who want to teach history for social justice, as well as possibilities for implementing more culturally relevant history pedagogy.

Caveats

Findings from a study of 100 children and adolescents in classroom and community settings can not be generalized to the historical and contemporary interpretations of young people in other communities. Demographic differences in socio-economic and/or racial-ethnic composition of the community and of relations between or among groups within the community might produce different outcomes. The students' and adults' rather fixed and bifurcated sense of their and others' racial identities as either "white" or "black" might not apply in settings where students' or adults' constructions of their and others' racial identities are more fluid and mixed (Lewis, 2003; Pollack, 2004). The findings also do not extend to classrooms in which teachers more directly, for more extended periods of time and/or more effectively, engaged students in difficult discussions around race and inequality (Bolgatz, 2005; Fine, 1993, 1995; Grant, 2003; Gutierrez, 2000).

Given theses caveats, however, there are several examples of "corraborative evidence" (Eisner, 1991) which suggest that the racial divide in children's, adolescents', and adults' historical and contemporary interpretations are not unique to the residents of Oakdale. One year, my graduate students and I collected data on eleventh graders in four other Michigan communities which varied demographically and by socio-economic status. We found similar race-related differences across contexts, although subtle differences emerged according to the degree of racial integration within the community and length of time that blacks had lived in the community. In addition, the dozen or so black undergraduate and graduate students who worked on the project came from different parts of the United States and their schooling experiences and social class backgrounds varied. Most however had constructed similarly critical interpretations of U.S. history and society and of the history they learned about in schools. For the past 10 years, I've taught at Hunter College in New York City and served as a student teacher supervisor. I've visited over 50 middle and high schools and repeatedly overheard students of color—specifically those who identify as African American and/or West Indian, Puerto Rican, Dominican, and/or Colombian—comment critically about the teaching of "white people's history" and lack equality in contemporary society.

The study did not examine the effects or effectiveness of particular curricular materials, instructional activities, or classroom interactions (see Fine, 1993; Bolgatz, 2005; Grant, 2003; Gutierrez, Rhymes & Larson, 1995; Gutierrez, 2000; Howard, 2004; Marri, 2005; Wills, 1994, 1996). Although teachers and texts which present more critical interpretations of the past might more capably connect with the interpretations of students of color and provide white students with more information about race and inequality, curricular infusion or transformation alone is not enough to enlist or broaden young people's interpretive frameworks or enable learning across socio-cultural differences. Studies that provide more finely grained analyses of the pedagogical approaches that result in more or less desirable outcomes in shaping young people's interpretive frames and views towards school history and citizenship may provide further evidence of the possibilities of and limitations to pedagogy aimed at social transformation.

Perhaps the greatest limitation of the study is that which is inherent in any project which portends to capture the "reality" of others' understandings. Like all researchers (Chase, 2005) my identity as a white, middle class professional and sense of myself as a "white ally" to black students and communities has left its imprint on this work. Although white and from a working class background, I differed from the white communities in Oakdale by having come from a family who saw professionalism as the road to status and security. I also adopted a more progressive political ideology than I found among most of Oakdale's white adolescents and adults. These differences might have led me to "read" the data with an overly critical eye, presenting whites' interpretations as overly "nationalistic" or accepting of school based accounts. And obviously, I differed from black participants along race and class lines; these differences might have led me to have read "black language" too literally and miss the more subtle meanings that black students and adults imparted through discourse (Lee, 2006).

For example, I am still searching for ways to capture the irony or sense of historical inversion implicit in many of the black students' interpretations. To suggest, as black students and parents had, that segregation was an example of "taxation without representation"; that "the only time when there has been full employment for black people was during slavery"; that "whites see blacks as lazy yet we're the ones who built the South"; or that "whites are afraid of black people but they're the ones who lynched us" seemed particularly insightful, even profound. I found less questioning and insight into history among white participants. Perhaps my white racial identity has so familiarized me with "white" or nationalist interpretations of history that I was tone deaf to white students', parents', or teachers' more interesting insights. Or maybe because whites are the dominant group whose experiences and views are reflected in schools and the broader culture, white youth and adults had less reason to question mainstream views. In any case, most readers may not be surprised to learn about racial differences in historical and political interpretations since individual and community knowledge and beliefs represented through language or discourse exist as a result of the historical and contemporary inequalities in power and race relations.

History of Oakdale

Oakdale's two centuries of history followed the pattern of other small towns and large cities in the Midwestern region of the country referred to as the Rust Belt. The governor of the Michigan territory opened the land to white settlement in 1819 and white male citizens gained the right to vote when Michigan became a state in 1837. The 1850 census recorded 971 people in the township of which Oakdale was a part, of whom 28 percent were black. Throughout the 1800s, many white men in Oakdale owned or rented land and employed black men as farmers or day laborers. White women assisted husbands and fathers with farming and domestic chores, while black women worked as domestics or servants in white households.

The township supported the first whites-only public school in 1843; by 1860, black residents had founded the township's first publicly supported "colored" school. While the township maintained segregated schools, some whites opened their homes to runaway slaves as part of the Underground Railroad. The majority of white male voters in the county voted for Lincoln and other Republicans in 1860 and scores of white and black men from the Oakdale area enlisted in the Union army. After the Civil War, many white and black service men returned to the area, only to be at odds again with the rise of racial hostility in the post-Civil War period.

Between 1900 and World War I, the growth of the automobile industry in and around Detroit changed Oakdale from a nineteenth-century farming community to a twentieth-century manufacturing city. The automobile industry recruited Southern whites and blacks to work in Michigan and during World War I, Southern blacks continued to move to the North to fill the manufacturing jobs left vacant by white men's entrance into the armed services. The influx of Southerners to Northern states, as well as post-World War I race riots spurred on by job competition between returning white veterans and more recently employed blacks led to an increase in racial conflict in and around Oakdale in the 1920s.

In one incident in the 1920s, the Ku Klux Klan marched through Oakdale's streets, threatening to burn down buildings which housed black businesses. As a result of increased racial tension, blacks organized a local chapter of the NAACP. When the local school board considered extending the segregated black elementary school beyond the first three grades, the NAACP chapter challenged the ruling in court and won. From that time on, all of the city's elementary schools were racially integrated.

With the outbreak of World War II, Henry Ford built an industrial assembly plant in Oakdale. Before the plant was completed, Oakdale had a population of 4,153 people; when the plant started operations in 1944, it supported 40,000 workers, many of whom were recruited from rural Kentucky and Tennessee. After World War II, thousands of workers left Oakdale to return to their former communities and by December, 1945, only 600 families remained. At the end of the war, Ford sold the assembly plant to another automobile manufacturer and by 1955, Oakdale's population had reached 12,000.

After World War II, the first blacks were elected and appointed to city- and county-wide public offices. During the Civil Rights Movement, the local NAACP chapter organized marches and boycotts for equal housing and job opportunities and residents in an adjacent city elected the first black mayor in 1972. The election did not represent a period of peaceful race relations, however. Black and white teachers and parents told stories of racial tensions in the schools, particularly during the 1970s. As black parents demanded greater decision making in school affairs, as well as more curricular content about African Americans, the Klu Klux Klan distributed literature outside the high school and threatened civil rights activists who picketed the schools. In the 1970s, the Ku Klux Klan tarred and feathered Oakdale's white high school principal for "caving in" to black demands. By the 1980s, the school district hired more black faculty and its first black school superintendent.

Although the decline in well paying industry and manufacturing jobs throughout the North, Midwest and South began after World War II (Sugrue, 1996), residents of Oakdale became particularly hard hit in the 1990s. In February, 1992, the automobile company which owned the assembly plant announced the plant's closing and laid off of 4,000 workers (Levin, 1993). Analysts predicted that the Oakdale school district would lose close to one million dollars a year and residents of Oakdale reported high levels of stress and illness as a result of the proposed closing (Dickerson, 1992; George, 1992; Harlan & Mitchell, 1992; Hernandez, 1992b). In April, 1992, county officials and the United Auto Workers sued the automaker to prevent the plant from closing, claiming that in exchange for tax abatements, the company promised to provide jobs until the year 2000. Despite the lawsuit, the assembly plant closed in July 1993. A few hundred workers relocated to another of the company's plants in Texas, while the majority of laid-off employees either left the community or found work as low- or semi-skilled laborers in local businesses (Fogel 1992, 1993; George, 1992; Hernandez, 1992a; Levin, 1992; Rimer, 1992).

The Community and Classrooms: 1990s

The 1990 and 2000 census described Oakdale as an urban fringe mid-sized city 30 miles from Detroit (U.S. Census Bureau, 1990, 2000). Of Oakdale's 18,500 residents in 1990, 70 percent were white, 27 percent were black, 1.6 percent were Hispanic, and less than 2 percent were Asian, American Indian, or other. By 2000, of the 18,545 residents, 61 percent were white, 32 percent were black, 2.1 percent were Hispanic, and less than 2 percent were designated as "some other race alone." The 2000 census also counted 4.8 percent of the school-age population as "of two or more races." The median household income was $32,000.00 in 1990 and $39,607 in 2000. In 1990, 42 percent of the adult population had high school degrees or one or more years of college, with another 12 percent having obtained a bachelor's or master's degree. In 2000, 45 percent of adults had graduated from high school or attended one or more years of college and 16 percent had college, master's, or doctoral degrees. Nine percent of the 6,300 households in 1990 lived below the poverty line; 13 percent of the district's 7,500 households lived below the poverty line in 2000.

The school district served 3,300 (1990) and 3,204 (2000) students in its five elementary schools, one middle school, and one high school (U.S. Census, 1990, 2000). In 1990, 64 percent of the student population was white, 31 percent black, 2.5 percent Hispanic and 2.5 percent was designated as Asian, American Indian, or "other." By 2000, 50 percent of the school age population was white, 42 percent black, 2.7 percent Hispanic, 2 percent was American Indian, Asian, or "some other race alone," and 3.3 percent was designated as belonging to more than one race. In 1990, about one-third of the students in the district were eligible for free lunches; by 2000, 38 percent were eligible. Over the decade, Oakdale's black population grew in proportion to the white population and these changes were evident in the schools, as greater percentages of black students populated Oakdale classrooms.

The statistical overview of Oakdale as a community populated by low paying unskilled and service sector adults was reflected in the town's mix of public buildings, private businesses, single family homes, apartment buildings and schools. When I drove around Oakdale, I was struck by the contrast between the adjacent upper middle class community, home to the University of Michigan (and myself) and the lower class community which educated Oakdale's youth. Oakdale's main street, called Main Street, housed small private businesses such as hairdressers, nail manicurists, wig sellers, and used auto parts and furniture rental stores, very different from the university town's main street, home to bookstores and upscale restaurants, coffee shops and boutiques. Although there were some well-to-do families and houses in town, single family houses in Oakdale averaged 700 square feet, most without basements, second floors or enclosed garages. One of the black graduate students said that the poorer houses in Oakdale reminded him of those of the poor black parts of towns in Mississippi, where his grandparents resided. The few public parks in Oakdale had worn out or broken swing sets and benches and served as hangouts for local gangs; "normal people," as one eleventh grader said, don't go to the parks, especially after dark.

Oakdale's five elementary schools, one middle school and one high school, like the public libraries and public buildings, were in better shape than many of the homes and parks. The schools and classrooms were built in the 1960s or later and were clean and in good repair. They were orderly, and had adequate numbers of adults in the building. It became apparent when entering school classrooms, however, that Oakdale schools lacked access to current materials and technology. I never saw a textbook in the schools that was newer than 1986; most additional materials such as classroom maps or other reading materials were provided by teachers from their own earnings. Each teacher had one outdated computer in his or her classroom and each school had one or two computer labs, with older and several broken Macs. Oakdale classrooms were not egregiously overcrowded: most had between 25 and 32 students per class and enough desks and chairs for each student. But they lacked up-to-date textbooks and library books, supplemental materials and almost no technological support. Like Oakdale homes and businesses, the schools were clean and relatively well maintained but lacked the kinds of text- and tool-rich environments that students and parents in middle class communities expected and had provided.

Consequently, teachers in Oakdale did what they could with limited materials and no computer access. The six teachers in the study bought many of the books and other learning materials such as maps, globes, and pamphlets which populated their classrooms, and students were encouraged to borrow books on the history of World War II or black inventors, for example. As evidenced in the following chapter, however, the teachers' intermittent teaching about white people's and the government's role in racism, contributions of people of color, and restrictions on rights led to mixed messages about the pervasiveness of racism and limits of democracy in U.S. history and society. In addition, the teachers' inability or unwillingness to engage students in frank discussions about the ubiquity of racism and limits of rights resulted in many missed opportunities for students to learn history for social justice.

Note

1 Throughout the book, I use the term white to describe European Americans and black to describe African Americans. I use these terms in part because they are shorter and less unwieldy and because the children, adolescents, and adults in the study most frequently referred to themselves and others in these terms. The vast majority of whites or European Americans in the study were of northern European descent (English, German, Irish, Scotch, Scandinavian) whose parents and grandparents had been born and raised in the Midwest or South. The vast majority of blacks or African Americans in the study had relatives who had moved from the South during the early to mid-1900s or had lived in the Midwest for one or more generations.

2

MIXED MESSAGES AND MISSED OPPORTUNITIES

Teachers' Perspectives and Pedagogies on Race and Rights in U.S. History

Like many school districts around the country, Oakdale public schools required students to complete United States history classes in the fifth, eighth and eleventh grades. Fifth grade teachers taught U.S. history from the beginning of human settlement through the Civil War; eighth and eleventh grade teachers taught chronological courses from the beginning of settlement through the Vietnam War. In addition, most teachers taught a unit on black history in February during Black History Month. During the period of the study, Michigan had a state social studies curriculum framework, but did not have standardized tests in social studies or other subjects. As a result, teachers had considerable discretion on what and how to teach about race and rights in history.

Despite the lack of state or district accountability, the teachers taught about the roles of racial groups and course of rights in U.S. history in similar ways. There was some variation, however, in the teachers' interpretations of race relations, particularly as they related to Native American-white relations, enslavement, segregation and the Civil Rights Movement. In addition, four of the teachers had teacher-centered styles where they did most of the talking in class and two were much more student-centered and encouraged student questions and discussions. When it came to lessons about race and rights in history and contemporary society, however, even the more student-centered teachers exerted control over student discourses in an effort to silence or close off potentially controversial or difficult conversations.

Table 2.1 Teachers' Pedagogies on Race/Rights in U.S. History and Pedagogical Styles

NAME AND GRADE	APPROACH TO RACIAL GROUPS	APPROACH TO RACE RELATIONS	APPROACH TO RIGHTS	TEACHER/ STUDENT CENTERED
Ms. Jensen – 5th grade	Whites as nation builders and racists Blacks primarily as victims[1] Native Americans as nation builders and victims	Racism and violence	Rights expanded Racism exists today	Teacher centered
Ms. Stone – 5th grade	Whites as nation builders Blacks primarily as victims Native Americans as nation builders	Racial cooperation	Rights expanded Equality exists today	Teacher centered
Mr. Bloch – 8th grade	Whites as nation builders Blacks primarily as victims Native Americans as nation builders	Racial cooperation	Rights expanded Equality and individual prejudice exist today	Teacher centered
Mr. Van Buren – 8th grade	Whites as nation builders Blacks primarily as victims Native Americans as nation builders and victims	Race relations as problem to be solved	Rights expanded Equality and individual prejudice exist today	Student centered
Ms. Hines – 11th grade	Whites as nation builders Blacks primarily as victims Native Americans as nation builders and victims	Race relations as problem to be solved	Rights expanded Equality and individual prejudice exist today	Teacher centered
Ms. Peabody – 11th grade	Whites as nation builders Blacks primarily as victims Native Americans as nation builders and victims	Race relations as problem to be solved	Rights expanded Equality and individual prejudice exist today	Student centered

* All teachers present blacks as subjects during the Underground Railroad and Civil Rights Movement

Beliefs vs. Practices: Teachers' Perspectives and Pedagogies on Racial Groups

The Presence and Absence of People of Color

When I asked the teachers about whether or why it was important to teach about racial groups, all said that it was necessary in a diverse society to teach children and adolescents about the contributions that people of different races and cultures had made to national development. Most concurred with Mr. Bloch, one of the eighth grade teachers that:

Students need to understand that all people—not just white people—contributed to the nation and who we are today. The fact that you have Native Americans, African Americans, European Americans, Asian Americans coming together in a particular area. Not always working together as we know, but everybody making their contributions in certain ways.

The teachers recognized that earlier conceptions of national history presented primarily as the product of elite white men were neither accurate nor beneficial to the education of future citizens in a democratic society. Ms. Hines, one of the eleventh grade teachers, commented that she took courses on African American history in graduate school in the early 1980s to supplement the traditional "dead white men's" history she had learned about in college. Having lived through the racial tensions in Oakdale schools in the 1970s, she thought that teaching and learning about black history might be one way to relieve racial tensions: "Black students deserve to learn more about their history and white students might get along better with blacks if they understood black history better, how black people made this nation great too."

Several teachers also conceptualized racial diversity as a concept that extended beyond black and white. Ms. Jensen, one of the fifth grade teachers, noted that elementary children knew nothing about Asians or Asian Americans in the U.S.:

When I've taught about Chinese people and the building of the trans-continental railroad, the children have been shocked to see Chinese people and culture there. I emphasize that it's a lot of different people who made the country. It's not important to me if they remember dates. What's important is that they understand that it is an entire world that created this country, not just one culture.

In my interviews with teachers, all emphasized the importance of teaching about racial and ethnic contributions to national history. In their classroom practices, however, most only discussed the contributions of black people during the Civil Rights Movement and those of Native Americans during the pre-colonial and colonial periods. When teaching about blacks in the nineteenth and twentieth centuries, the teachers occasionally discussed black agency in resisting enslavement or segregation and described black victimization, but they never described the contributions that black people made to the national economy, polity, society or culture until the Civil Rights Movement. Similarly, the teachers discussed Native American assistance to early European settlers but made no mention of their contributions to economic, political or social life beyond these initial encounters. More often, when the teachers taught about blacks and Native Americans, they presented them as enslaved or segregated victims of Southerners or the government, but rarely as a collective people who contributed positively to national development. Consequently, the teachers' instruction contributed to white and black students' understanding of Native Americans and blacks as victims but little to their knowledge about their roles as nation builders.

Mr. Bloch was the only teacher to include lessons on people of color other than blacks and Native Americans (Mexican Americans in the Civil Rights Movement) and despite Ms. Jensen's comments about the importance of Asian Americans, she had no lessons on their experiences. Mr. Van Buren, the other eighth grade teacher, reminded students during a lesson on the Civil Rights Movement that Asians, not blacks or whites, were the most populous race in the world and young people needed to learn about their contributions and experiences. "It wasn't just black people who lacked rights," Mr. Van Buren affirmed. But he never presented any lessons on Asian Americans or on any group besides blacks and Native Americans. Overall, the teachers provided mixed messages about the role of people of color in history: in interviews and occasionally in class, they emphasized the significance of teaching about the contributions of diverse racial groups. In practice, however, the teachers rarely included lessons on people other than blacks and Native Americans and they most often presented them as victims rather than nation builders.

The Absence and Presence of Whites

When talking in interviews about the importance of racial groups historically, none of the teachers discussed whites as people who contributed to national development, yet all of the teachers taught about white actors and groups as the main agents of historical change and development. All of the teachers attributed the nation's democratic foundation to white colonists and founding fathers. They credited them with winning a revolution which "gave us our freedom" and creating a Constitution and Bill of Rights which "gave us laws and rights and the freedoms we have today." Even as the teachers denounced the "extra credit" that elite white men had received from historians for national development, they taught through texts and activities that elite white men provided the formation and foundation of the nation, which led to the freedom and rights that Americans enjoy today.

The eighth and eleventh grade teachers also depicted late nineteenth- and early twentieth-century European immigration as a positive contribution to the nation's economic development and ethnic diversity. They presented European immigrants as having overcome tremendous obstacles to become "part of the American dream," as Ms. Hines asserted. "If it weren't for immigrants," Mr. Bloch announced, "we wouldn't be here today and America would not be what it is today." Mr. Van Buren compared immigrants to nineteenth-century blacks and then credited immigrants with having modernized and diversified the country:

> Like blacks, the establishment looked down on immigrants, thought they were a lesser breed and treated them like second-class citizens. They started organizations to end immigration and even tried to outlaw immigrants from having kids. But eventually, immigrants became accepted, if not in the first generation, then in the second or third. And look what they did for this country ... built and worked in the factories and lived in tenements and worked their way up to what they have today. Back then, when the Irish came over, the Jews came over, the Americans already here didn't like it. But we learned better as a nation how to accept people of different backgrounds.

Ms. Hines, one of the eleventh grade teachers, described the contributions that European immigrants made to the nation's diversity by overcoming discrimination and creating a melting pot that paved the way for future generations:

> When the immigrants came over, there was a lot of discrimination. They couldn't get good jobs and it was dangerous in factories ... lived in ghettos

and their children went to work and couldn't go to school. But they made this country a better place … came from all different places and added diversity to the nation and not just English and Germans were here … They made America a melting pot for everybody, where everybody from all over the world came. And we see this today too, that people are still coming and if not always accepted, they still come to get better jobs and things for their kids and add to diversity.

Like Ms. Hines, the other teachers believed it was important to teach about the contributions of people of color; in practice, however, they presented only whites as the significant shapers of national development. The teachers positioned elite white men as the nation's founders who created and extended democracy and white immigrants as those who rose above discrimination to build an infrastructure and contribute to cultural diversity. They rarely credited people of color with similar achievements or accolades; only when teaching about the Underground Railroad and Civil Rights Movement did teachers present lessons on black contributions to national life.

Ms. Jensen was the only teacher whom I interviewed who raised white racism as an important and enduring aspect of national history. Her understanding, she said, stemmed from the fact that she married an African American man and had bi-racial children. She believed that all children needed awareness of the historical legacy of racism so that slavery and legal segregation wouldn't happen again:

Children have to know what happened in the past, things like slavery and segregation and how the government put Native Americans and Japanese people in camps. And there was racism in the North and the South; it wasn't just in the South. There were lynchings, riots, cross burnings in the North. There's a history of white people in the North committing crimes against blacks and others. I don't want to give them too much of this, but I want to make them aware. Not to let these things happen again, so that we don't commit the same crimes or at least be aware of it.

As shown in the section on race relations, Ms. Jensen discussed racism and white violence not only during slavery, but during the Civil Rights

Movement and sporadically throughout the curriculum. The other teachers mentioned discrimination or "racial problems" in the past. But they did not associate whites with racism or racism as a systematic and ongoing aspect of the nation's legacy.

Critique

The teachers communicated mixed messages about the significance of people of color in national history. They believed in teaching about the experiences of the racial/ethnic groups that comprised the nation's population and knew that their students hadn't received much instruction about the experiences of people other than blacks and whites. But they taught very little about any groups other than blacks or whites, and only presented blacks as having contributed to national development during the Underground Railroad and Civil Rights Movement. Instead, they taught mostly about white leaders and European immigrants as nation builders who contributed to economic and political development and diversified the ethnic composition of the nation. And as evidenced in their classroom discussions about race relations discussed later on in the chapter, they minimized or ignored whites' responsibility or accountability for racism as a national, rather than just Southern, phenomena.

In addition, most of the teachers had taken traditional history survey courses in college and used outdated history textbooks which contained little information on the agency of people of color. None had taken courses in their teacher education programs or had had professional development workshops which encouraged them to reflect on the dichotomies between their pedagogical beliefs and practices. All of the teachers were raised in all-white communities and, except for Ms. Jensen, lacked interactions with people of color who might have had different knowledge and beliefs about the role of race and rights in history and contemporary society. The teachers' limited exposure to the latest historical scholarship, professional development experiences, and interactions with people whose interpretive frameworks differed from their own constrained their awareness of the difference between their pedagogical beliefs and practices, as well as their knowledge about the contributions of people of color.

Heroic Individuals of Color Approach to Racial Groups

Mr. Bloch was the only teacher who included a week's worth of lessons about racial groups other than whites and blacks. In teaching about the Civil Rights Movement, he organized a unit on Cesar Chavez as a great leader who changed history and he often compared his actions with those of Martin Luther King, Jr. Mr. Bloch started the unit by asking students what they thought was worth protesting for or against today. Without waiting for answers, he emphasized that is was important for young people "to be proud of who you are and all that you can be. If you believe in something, you should stand up for it." He gave a lecture about the difference that an individual can make historically and today and cited the accomplishments of Martin Luther King, Jr. and Ghandi. He emphasized their beliefs in non-violence, democracy and "including all races in their struggles for freedom." He ended the lecture by stating that during the next few days, they would study how King inspired other leaders to fight for equal rights for "all people."

The following two days, the students watched and answered questions on a video about Cesar Chavez and his work with migrant farm workers. When the video ended, Mr. Bloch noted how Cesar Chavez, like King, was a courageous leader who organized grape boycotts. He did this "to help his people gain economic rights. He taught us that consumers can stand up and don't buy grapes. This will lead to a surplus and the farm owners won't make money and force them to give the farm workers better wages." Mr. Bloch again reiterated the significance of the individual when he then passed out a handout entitled, "No Grapes" and asked students to think about the last paragraph:

> Even though many think prejudice will always exist, that may be true. However, if you educate yourself and remember not to judge people from their appearances, beliefs, or gender, then you can be one less person to pass on prejudices to future generations. This is how we can all make a difference.

Critique

Mr. Bloch's focus on the Mexican American civil rights struggle of the 1960s provided important lessons for students about the power of the individual within the context of organized resistance, as well as the means people have used to challenge inequality. At the same time, he framed the lessons around the action of a great leader and about the individual's choice to boycott grapes, rather than the contributions that thousands of Mexican and Mexican American farm workers had made to organized resistance. He provided a mixed message about the role of individual heroes who come along once in a millennium and barely credited the thousands who fought alongside Chavez and without whom Chavez could not have been successful. By having over-emphasized the roles of charismatic leaders and individual consumer choice, and having under-emphasized the power of Mexican and Mexican American farm workers as a group, Mr. Bloch missed an opportunity to demonstrate the contributions that thousands of people of color had made to issues around economic rights.

Teachers' Perspectives and Pedagogies about Rights

The teachers described the Constitution as having laid the foundation for national government and the Bill of Rights as having guaranteed individual rights which Americans enjoy today. But each also raised the restrictive nature of rights in early America. Several times, Ms. Stone told her fifth graders, "I hope you don't leave my class without knowing that rich white men wrote the Bill of Rights. No poor farmers, no women, no African Americans or Native Americans, they had to be white male land owners." Ms. Hines similarly explained the Bill of Rights to her eleventh graders as a document which both ensures Americans' rights today but applied only to white men originally. She also gave a short lecture on how people like Martin Luther King, Jr., and others used the Constitution to argue for expanded rights for all. She concluded by noting:

> Americans have the rule of law to fight for equal rights and dignity. We
> are a country founded on the rule of law and although not everyone had

rights, more and more people, like women and blacks, got their rights. Now you see blacks and women in Congress and in state governments, and that was unimaginable 100 years ago.

Mr. Bloch, Mr. Van Buren and Ms. Peabody also emphasized the original limits of rights to wealthy white men in early America but reiterated that the Bill of Rights laid the foundation for "everyone's rights" (Mr. Bloch) or the "rights we have today" (Mr. Van Buren). Mr. Bloch instructed that over time, Americans came to believe that more people should have rights and "more and more people started getting equal rights, especially during the Jackson presidency." When a black eighth grader remarked that slaves didn't receive rights, Mr. Bloch explained:

> The Constitution allowed slavery and did not acknowledge African Americans or women as citizens. Many of the founding fathers had problems with the establishment of slavery in the Constitution. But we've always had problems and we've always come up with solutions. They might not have been able to change the Constitution that day, but they worked on it and we've continued to grow and prosper.

Mr. Van Buren and Ms. Peabody took a slightly different approach to Constitutional history and its applicability to contemporary society. Mr. Van Buren interpreted the American Revolution and subsequent conflicts over nation building in terms of economic or class interests. "Powerful New England merchants had different economic interests than Southern plantation owners," Mr. Van Buren explained, and each set of actors wanted their interests represented in the new government and Constitution. Conflicts and compromises among powerful interest groups, Mr. Van Buren asserted, explained why the Constitution included provisions in which black slaves counted as three-fifths of a person for Congressional representation and why large and small states had proportional representation in the House of Representatives and equal representation in the Senate.

Mr. Van Buren and Ms. Peabody also taught that the Bill of Rights was written as a response to colonial constraint under British rule and not just as a mechanism to disburse rights equally to all. "Only white men with property could vote," Mr. Van Buren restated throughout the week, "and blacks, women, and ordinary people couldn't vote and rarely participated in politics. People today take voting for granted, but every group had to work hard to gain the right to vote." To make his point, he cited the election of Andrew Jackson as having opened the franchise to landless white men; the thirteenth, fourteenth, and fifteenth amendments as having extended in principle voting rights to black men; the nineteenth amendment as having given women the right to vote; and the Civil Rights Movement as having put "the teeth into the Civil War amendments." Yet even Mr. Van Buren credited and identified with the nation as a positive and inclusive democratic entity:

> that's why everybody continues to buy into the democracy that we have because they see that nothing stays the same. We're always on the cutting edge and willing to do what's right; it's a symbol that we're a nation that is willing to accept change.

Critique

Despite the teachers' discourses about the mixed legacy of the Constitution as a historic document which gave rights to a minority and excluded the majority, none of the classroom activities on the Constitution or Bill of Rights referred to their exclusive nature. Ms. Jensen began her two-day unit on the Constitution by having fifth graders create their own school-wide Constitution; Ms. Stone had fifth graders work in groups to explain in their own words an edited version of the Bill of Rights. The eighth and eleventh grade teachers spent considerable time on exercises in which students elaborated on the separation of powers and checks and balances. Mr. Bloch drilled his eighth grade students on which branch of government had the power to check or curtail the power of another and told students that it was the "brilliance of the founding fathers" to create a government in which no branch had unchecked powers. The eleventh grade teachers also gave students hypothetical cases which questioned people's right to free speech and students defended whether the relevant amendment applied. Although the teachers critiqued the traditional historical narrative about the universal nature of rights and unfettered spread of democracy, they provided no activities to reinforce themes about exclusion and inequality.

Rather than use the contradictions of the founding documents as an opening to examine race, gender, or class hierarchies, the teachers retreated to traditional lessons about governmental structure and operations. A lesson, for example, on the Constitutional compromise that counted enslaved African Americans as three-fifths of a person would have reinforced the limits of democracy and beliefs in racial superiority. Or lessons on Northern enslaved and free blacks' petitions to state legislatures for freedom or repatriation to Africa would have demonstrated that racism and slavery weren't confined to the South and that enslaved and free blacks turned democracy on its head by petitioning for their freedom. Because the teachers privileged themes about expanding democracy and provided mixed messages about the extent of exclusion in early national history, white and black students selected instructional messages which reinforced rather than challenged their pre-existing beliefs about democracy and exclusion.

Teachers' Perspectives and Pedagogies on Race Relations: Three Frameworks

Race Relations as Cooperation

While the teachers taught about rights in early national history in a relatively uniform way, they had different approaches to teaching about race relations. Ms. Stone (fifth grade) and Mr. Bloch (eighth grade) recognized and occasionally taught about racial conflict but mainly focused on racial cooperation. They thought this would be the best way to minimize racial tensions in their classrooms and the community and that racism no longer was a problem in contemporary society. Mr. Bloch also emphasized cooperation as a means to shape student behavior. By showing how people in history cooperated to reach goals, he hoped that his students would learn lessons about resolving conflicts peacefully. "I try to show the kids that there are better ways to solve problems than name calling, and fighting is not the way we should treat each other."

Ms. Stone thought that racial harmony or tolerance best could be accomplished by presenting a "balanced perspective" on race relations. When asked what she meant, she emphasized "the importance of tempering the negative with the positive":

I think it's important in a community like this to emphasize the positive, how people from different races or religions got along and helped each other out. They get enough about differences and problems from the media and their own families. Part of my job is to show them that yes, bad things happened here, but not all people were bad and some people actually tried to make things better.

When asked for further explanation, Ms. Stone referred specifically to the black community and the need to teach black children about white efforts to end slavery and segregation. "There is a lot of anger in the black community," Ms. Stone commented, "and I think this is one of the ways to smooth things out by saying that not all people were bad."

An example of instruction about racial cooperation occurred at the beginning of the year. In presenting Native Americans, Ms. Stone and Mr. Bloch credited Native Americans with having been the "first Americans." Both said it was important to dispel the myth that Europeans discovered America; "Native Americans," Mr. Bloch insisted, "should get credit for being here first." After having examined the similarities and differences among Native American tribes, both teachers included lessons on how Native Americans helped European explorers and settlers. Ms. Stone reminded students that Native Americans helped settlers by giving them food during their first winters and this became the genesis of Thanksgiving. Mr. Bloch also highlighted that European settlers would not have made it through their first years in North America had they not received food and learned agricultural techniques from Native Americans. He also focused on trade between the two groups, noting that both sides "gained something they wanted from each other ... how helping each other out, not fighting, was beneficial to both sides."

Neither teacher mentioned conflict between Native Americans and settlers during the early colonial period. Ms. Stone thought it was unnecessary to teach about the negative impact of European settlement on Native American civilizations because the major problems between Native Americans and European Americans occurred in the late nineteenth century. She also thought it was important for children to recognize that the "country wouldn't be what it is today without Europeans." Mr. Bloch, on the other hand, emphasized racial cooperation because he wanted students to see alternatives to racial conflict. "There's too much emphasis on conflict … the kids have to learn how people of different races have worked together and helped each other … maybe not all the time, but sometimes."

During the lessons, it was difficult to assess what students in either classroom had learned about Native American–white relations. Both teachers organized most of their lessons on Native Americans around the differences among Native American tribes and none included any activities or discussion which examined Native American-white relations. They also did not encourage discussion and expected children to accept and reiterate teacher explanations of historical actors and events, especially when it involved lessons about race. During a unit on European exploration, for example, Ms. Stone mentioned that "fights broke out" between Native Americans and settlers and "settlers slowly pushed the Native Americans off the land." When a black student commented that "it wasn't fair," Ms. Stone concurred, "it wasn't fair, but here, we're learning about how different people got along." At the end of the year, white children incorporated Ms. Stone's lessons about Native American assistance to whites and only one referred to racial conflict; conversely, three black children referred to racial conflict ("whites kicked them off their land") and only one child mentioned "they helped the white people with food and stuff."

Ms. Stone also taught about enslavement as an example of positive race relations. She began the unit by explaining the Atlantic slave trade as an international system in which Europeans sailed to the west coast of Africa and transported Africans to the Americas for trade or labor. Students filled out a map of the routes of the triangular slave trade and discussed a well known drawing of a slave cargo ship in which enslaved people were chained together like sardines. The drawing, along with their textbook readings about some of the horrors of the Middle Passage, disturbed white and black children. In discussing the picture and passage, one black girl commented that "slavery was wrong, it wasn't fair" and a white boy asked "why were people so mean to slaves?" In response, Ms. Stone explained that although today people can grasp the inhumanity of slavery, people of the time didn't see things that way. She also commented that not all masters were terrible. She told the children that:

Yes, there were a lot of people who were very bad but there were also ones (slave owners) who were very good. They were slaves and that was their role. This was not seen as wrong as we think it is now; that was the way things were at that time. Some people treated them very well and some didn't.

Critique

Ms. Stone began her lessons on enslavement by including examples of the inhumane aspects of the Middle Passage. But her desire to focus on cooperation by teaching about good white slave owners presented mixed messages about the role of whites in racial oppression. Instead of presenting slavery in the U.S. as an oppressive institution which benefited whites and debased blacks and whites, she focused on individual paternalistic relationships between the enslaved and slave owners. If she wanted to discuss racial cooperation during slavery, it would have made more sense to have discussed interracial cooperation to disrupt and abolish slavery, i.e. the cooperation of blacks and whites in the Underground Railroad or other aspects of the abolitionist movement. Teaching about individual acts of kindness also was offensive to the legacy of slavery. It might have given black children who began and ended the year with knowledge about racial violence during slavery reason to dismiss her pedagogy about race. And white children could have learned misguided lessons that individual instances of kindness, rather than institutional structures, are ways to measure historical or contemporary relations.

Civil Rights Movement

While only Ms. Stone discussed racial cooperation during enslavement, she, Mr. Bloch (eighth grade) and Ms. Hines (eleventh grade) focused on racial cooperation during the Civil Rights Movement. The three teachers wanted their students to know that whites as well as blacks participated in protests and they emphasized that civil rights leaders established rights for all dispossessed peoples. Mr. Bloch noted that the movement fulfilled the promise that "all men are created equal, it doesn't matter what color or religion you are." The teachers believed that by emphasizing the multi-racial composition and benefits of the Civil Rights Movement, white children might learn how they could stand up for "what's right" (Ms. Hines) and black students might feel less anger towards society and white people in general (Ms. Stone and Mr. Bloch). When I asked about teaching about racial conflict, all three said they downplayed violence because it might inflame black students. They didn't mention the effects that the lessons might have on white children.

In teaching about multiracial cooperation, Ms. Stone showed a filmstrip on the March on Washington and pointed out the multiracial composition of the marchers. She also emphasized that continuous acts of nonviolent civil disobedience were successful and these eventually led to the desegregation of public facilities and equal rights for all minorities and women. She provided very little classroom time to discuss these issues and had little sense of the effects the lessons might have had on children's understandings. When she once asked students how the Civil Rights Movement affected their lives, white and black children said that they "now attend school together" and "anybody" (white students) or "you" (black students) can visit any restaurant or restroom. When one black girl suggested that civil rights leaders were role models for blacks, Ms. Stone responded that civil rights leaders "helped all people, not just black people."

Mr. Bloch began the unit by teaching that it was about "getting together and saying that we Americans made some steps but now we have to push harder to take more steps so that freedoms are ensured. We felt great about ourselves up to the 1950s and 1960s, with the exception of the Civil Rights Movement. So people went out and made a change." He and Ms. Hines began with some of the traditional lessons of the Civil Rights Movement: the landmark *Brown vs. Board of Education* decision, Rosa Parks' refusal to move to the back of the bus, and King's "I Have a Dream Speech." Both also were intent on showing interracial cooperation. Ms. Hines did this by showing passages of the March on Washington from *Eyes on the Prize* and asking students to comment on the multiracial composition of the demonstration. Mr. Bloch showed a video on Cesar Chavez and the United Farm Workers. He told students that "Mexicans like Chavez and his organization fought for rights too; it wasn't just about blacks fighting for equality; there were lots of people who weren't treated fairly and they went out and did something about it."

Mr. Bloch and Ms. Hines also emphasized that civil rights activities led to the desegregation of public facilities and the acquisition of equal rights for all Americans. "It wasn't just a movement for black people, Ms. Hines asserted,

> Martin Luther King, Jr. wanted rights for everyone. Black people, Hispanics, Asian Americans … the point was to make things better for everyone, that everyone deserved equal rights and respect. Women too got ahead during this time … they could be in sports, do jobs like medicine and law … everyone benefited from civil rights.

Mr. Bloch similarly ended the unit on the Civil Rights Movement by noting not just how much the nation had grown, but how far Oakdale as a community had come. He reminded his students that

> although things still aren't equal, we've come a long way. When I started teaching in the 1970s, there was a lot of racial tension and white and black students had to be separated in the cafeteria … sometimes fights broke out at football games. Now we don't see this happening much. You sit side by side in the classroom and on sports teams, I see people walking in the halls together. Things have come a long way.

Critique

Mr. Bloch and Ms. Hines made an important point by telling students about the multiracial composition and effects of the Civil Rights Movement. White and black eighth and eleventh graders came to class with knowledge about black people's roles as agents and beneficiaries of the movement, but not with an understanding that the Civil Rights Movement included or benefited others. By highlighting white cooperation and minimizing white violence, however, the teachers didn't present the strength and viciousness of white resistance and how difficult it was to overcome. They gave very limited examples of interracial cooperation and overstated the movement's effects in obtaining equal rights for blacks. Voting rights and desegregation of public facilities were important victories of the Civil Rights Movement and resulted in policies and practices which created significant change. But it did not lead to racial equality and by not discussing what the movement did not accomplish, the teachers didn't provide a framework for the existence of racism in contemporary society.

In addition, the teachers were unaware of their students' prior knowledge or preconceptions of the Civil Rights Movement. White and black eighth and eleventh graders started the year conceiving of the Civil Rights Movement as a movement by and for black people, and black students associated the movement with racial conflict and black pride. The teachers could have built on students' preconceptions by having affirmed the major role that blacks played in the movement, discussed white resistance and then presented whites as allies, rather than as equal players. Instead, they ignored, shut down or contradicted students' views of the Civil Rights Movement as a movement of great importance to and about the black community, underemphasized the role of white resistance to black civil rights, and did not discuss the limitations on rights on people of color today.

Race Relations as Conflict and Violence

Ms. Jensen, the fifth grade teacher, often discussed racial conflict and violence when teaching about race relations in history. She thought it was important for her students to see the connection between past and present and recognize the ongoing legacy of racism. Having grown up in Texas and traveled around the South, Ms. Jensen said that she figured out in middle school that "even though I was told everyone was equal, I saw and witnessed that everyone was not treated equally. I've seen slavery in the South in the 1960s; I've seen nooses in trees." She moved to Michigan to attend college and never returned to the South. In the North, she learned that "racism is a little more subtle, but it's still there. The black children are aware of it, but I'm not sure the white kids think much about it." Ms. Jensen's view on race and teaching about race relations also had been influenced by her marriage to a black man and having two biracial children. "It's a matter of balance; my own kids have to know that they are from both cultures and we support both cultures."

In teaching about Native Americans, Ms. Jensen emphasized the differences among Native American tribes and her students spent a week making clay dioramas which highlighted differences in homes, agriculture and hunting, and tools. Ms. Jensen also talked about conflicts between Native Americans and Europeans and then Americans. She began by explaining that not only had European settlers taken land from the Native Americans, they also tried to enslave them:

> First whites tried to make Native Americans slaves but they knew the land so it was easy for them to escape. That's when they turned to Africa and Africans. It was much harder for African slaves to escape into the forests and swamps in America because they didn't know the land and they spoke many different languages.

In teaching about enslavement, Ms. Jensen talked about the African slave trade, the Middle Passage and the racism inherent in a forced labor system. She explained to the students that

> the Europeans went in and snatched people out and brought them here or other places to do the labor. Africans were packed onto boats, chained together and not allowed to wash or use toilets and beaten if they complained. Many were terrified because they didn't know what was happening to them. Once they got here, they were sold into slavery. They not only had to work for the owners and were beaten; slaves were considered the property of whites.

She passed out the drawing of Africans packed into the hull of a slave ship and she and students commented on the inhumanity of the experience. Students then read a story about the *Amistad* rebellion and white and black students expressed concern about the violence directed towards Africans. Ms. Jensen used the opportunity to explain how many enslaved people did not acquiesce to enslavement but fought against it in overt or covert ways. She explained how "house or field slaves" might do their work more slowly as an act of resistance or pretend they didn't understand something to be released from responsibilities. Throughout the unit on enslavement, and particularly when they read about the harshness of the work conditions in their textbooks, white and black children expressed anger or indignation at the "unfairness" of enslavement. Ms. Jensen tried to channel the children's concerns about abusive race relations by having students read a story about the *Amistad* slave rebellion which described Africans who took over a slave ship and later won their freedom. When I asked her about the lesson, which I didn't observe, she said

> We read quietly on our own first and then they got into groups to discuss it. A lot of students were very upset after they read this. So we did spend a lot of time on this. Even my white students were shocked that children on the ship would be treated so poorly. I also urged them to see the movie when it came out. "It's your parent's decision," I tell them, "because it's very ugly and it's not pretty, it's not a film you're going to rest easy on." But a lot of black kids have seen another movie, *Rosewood.* So they were already knowledgeable about some of the violence that African Americans have faced and how they have defended themselves.

When asked if 10-year-old children could handle learning about racial violence, Ms. Jensen responded:

> I think many of the black children hear about these things at home and it's important for all children to know the history of race relations, that slavery wasn't just wrong, it was violent, took away people's dignity … But they also need to know that slaves fought against it; they didn't just accept it, like 'this is our life and we have to make it the best we can.' Some thought like that, but others found ways to change their situation.
>
> I'd also like for them to try to recognize that if slavery hadn't happened, then maybe we wouldn't be here. But there could have been another way without hurting cultures or people. I don't want to give them too much of this, but I want to make them aware. And how not to let slavery happen again, make sure you know everything about it so that it doesn't happen again, so that they don't commit the same crimes or at least are aware of it.

In discussing the Civil Rights Movement Ms. Jensen openly discussed white racial resistance and violence towards blacks. She presented the movement as a time when blacks in the South and North still struggled against violence and unequal treatment under the law. She discussed the protests and arrests of Rosa Parks and Martin Luther King, Jr. as means to end segregation, attain equal rights and promote black pride and community empowerment. She spent considerable time discussing the "dignity" of Parks and King during their arrests and subsequent activities, and brought up the morality and courage of their stances in the face of racist individuals and institutions. She also emphasized that ordinary people participated in civil rights, sacrificed and showed courage during the Civil Rights Movement and the movement "could not have been won" without the participation of thousands of people. In addition to reading their textbooks, students read a story about Martin Luther King, Jr., which included phone calls of death threats directed at King and mentioned the bombing of King's home in Atlanta. Ms. Jensen did most of the talking during the unit, however, and although the black children reflected lessons about racial violence and civil rights leaders' courage at the end of the year, the white children did not reflect these themes.

Critique

Unlike the other teachers in the study, Ms. Jensen was not afraid to raise issues about racial conflict and violence, even with elementary children. She provided clear messages about the role of racism in the nation's development and considered the significance of white and black children learning about the nation's legacy of racism and black people's resistance to slavery. Her decision to do so was educative: she believed white and black children needed to learn about the nation's abuses so that they would become vigilant citizens in the future. And at the end of the year, her emphasis on racial conflict made some difference: black children discussed conflict in their end-of-the-year explanations between Native Americans, and both white and black children represented slavery at the end of the year as a cruel and inhumane institution which included beatings and whippings. Some children also made reference to slave resistance by noting that some ran away or "didn't do their chores." And both black and white children talked about the "unfairness" of slavery.

Like the other teachers, however, Ms. Jensen didn't provide much class time for discussion, especially about how racism might still affect people of color today or what people in contemporary society can do to ensure that the "same types of crimes" don't happen again. She might have asked students about how people of color today are treated and white students might have learned about problems that black children face as a result of racism. She also could have included stories about the existence of racism today and asked students to examine and discuss how people of color, as well as whites, have worked together to challenge inequality. Ms. Hines presented many good examples of racism historically, was aware of how racism affected black children in her class and believed in the importance of having all children learn about racism's legacy. But she missed opportunities to engage her students in discussions about their own or their families' experiences, and/or how the children themselves, as well as adults, could challenge "unfair" or discriminatory practices.

Race Relations as a "Problem" to be Solved

Mr. Van Buren (eighth grade), Ms. Peabody (eleventh grade) and at times Ms. Hines (eleventh grade) taught about race relations as a problem to be solved. They presented the problem of race as something that the founding fathers had left unresolved in the framing of the new nation. "As time went on," Ms. Peabody explained to the class at the beginning of the year, "Americans as a nation faced the problems of racial inequality." In presenting Native Americans as the "first Americans," the teachers emphasized variations among tribes based on geography. They also referred to Native American and white conflict, or as Mr. Van Buren expressed it, they "ran into problems" as whites took over more and more Native American land. The teachers, however, did not explore the issue of Native American-white conflict in colonial or the early national period, however. Instead, they noted that the classes would revisit the problem of Native American-white relations in the late nineteenth century, when, as Ms. Hines explained, "the tragedy of Native American civilizations" took center stage.

In teaching about the westward movement of whites across the continent after the Civil War, Mr. Van Buren announced the migration "was an opportunity and a tragedy." He then asked students what he meant by this. Students commented that westward migration gave opportunities to land-hungry Easterners, but they were stumped on what he meant by the tragedy of migration. Mr. Van Buren reminded students that he had told them at the beginning of the year that after the Civil War, Native Americans and whites "ran into trouble." "The problem," Mr. Van Buren reminded students, was that one's man's opportunity was another one's misfortune.

Americans wanted land for farming and the Native Americans in the west used the land for hunting buffalo. This led to a conflict ... especially as more and more immigrants came to the East. The solution for some Americans was to move west and get land. But the solution for some was a problem for the Native Americans, who lost their traditional ways of living ...

Ms. Hines and Ms. Peabody also emphasized that the westward movement created conflicts between Americans who wanted to use the land for farming or grazing and Native Americans who followed the buffalo and moved from place to place. Ms. Peabody showed a video on the Battle of Wounded Knee, commenting that the army massacred Native Americans at Wounded Knee in part to avenge Custer's death. All of the teachers criticized the concept of manifest destiny, which convinced Americans that Native Americans were an inferior race and Americans had a God-given duty to "populate the land from sea to sea." They also presented the decimation of Native American populations and removal to reservations as morally reprehensible acts. Only Ms. Peabody discussed how the government created and participated in policies and practices of racial superiority and the endless round of government treaty making and breaking with Native Americans. Mr. Van Buren ended a two-day lesson on Native American removal to reservations by noting, "this was one problem the government didn't handle well. We took the Native American lands and gave them almost nothing in return. It's a shameful part of our history."

In teaching about enslavement, Mr. Van Buren, Ms. Hines and Ms. Peabody began their units with the international dimensions of the slave trade and maps which illustrated the routes of trade. Each teacher mentioned but did not focus on the physical abuse of the enslaved on slave ships and plantations and white people's general acceptance of slavery. Ms. Hines and Ms. Peabody passed out edited documents on the slave codes which detailed restrictions on slaves' activities and punishments for enslaved people who disobeyed the codes. After some of the black students commented on the harshness of the codes, Ms. Hines emphasized that slavery "was around from the beginning of time ... it was not new or unique to European countries." She also included that Africans participated in the slave trade and the European slave trade could not have been as successful as it was without the willingness of African kings and tribal leaders. Some of the black students shook their heads in disbelief and one commented, "black people didn't make black people pick their cotton or clean up after their kids." Ms. Hines ignored the comment.

The teachers also discussed black resistance to slavery. Ms. Peabody suggested that "slaves didn't deal with their problems by just taking it ... thousands escaped from slavery" and those who remained "created a culture that helped them cope with being slaves." Ms. Peabody discussed the covert ways that blacks resisted enslavement, like participating in work slowdowns, pretending ignorance and poisoning the master's food. The three teachers included lessons on the Underground Railroad and the participation of blacks and whites in abolitionism. Ms. Hines noted that "whites and blacks worked together to solve the problem." Mr. Van Buren stressed that even though the Emancipation Proclamation did not free a single slave, the document signaled that there were "people in the government who supported African American rights and freedoms. They understood that slavery was a problem ... it was wrong."

Mr. Van Buren began his unit on the Civil Rights Movement by noting it was about "getting together and saying that we Americans made some steps but now we have to push harder to take more steps so that freedoms are ensured. We felt great about ourselves up to the 1950s and 1960s, with the exception of the Civil Rights Movement." Ms. Hines began the unit by noting that even though blacks had been freed 100 years before, segregation was a political problem and moral dilemma. She reminded students about Jim Crow laws and policies which excluded blacks from voting and regarded segregation as "morally wrong." Ms. Hines told her students that the

> Civil Rights Movement solved a lot of problems. There was the problem of blacks in the South who couldn't vote or have freedom of speech, there was the problem of Mexican Americans who didn't have rights, ... women, disabled people didn't have many rights either. The Civil Rights Movement dealt with the problems of a lot of people and it gave people rights. It made America live up to its promises ... many people got together to make this happen.

Ms. Hines and Mr. Van Buren taught many of the traditional lessons on the Civil Rights Movement: Rosa Parks' refusal to move to the back of the bus and the success of the Montgomery Bus Boycott; Southerners' hostility to civil rights activists who participated in sit-ins and freedom rides and the courage of those who participated; and Martin Luther King's March on Washington and the "I Have a Dream Speech." The teachers focused on how people "got together to solve the problems of discrimination" (Ms. Hines) and each emphasized that the movement led to the extension of rights to people of all races, religions and nationalities. Mr. Van Buren ended the unit by noting not just how much the nation had grown, but how far Oakdale as a community had come. He reminded his students that "although things still aren't equal, we've come a long way." The changes that occurred as a result of the Civil Rights Movement, he said, were a testament to Americans' abilities to face and solve problems:

> We had segregation in the South thirty years ago. We're still working on that problem; we're still trying to solve things. But that's what this nation is all about. Nothing is going to stand still, it's constantly growing and changing, constantly trying to work out its flaws.

Critique

In teaching about race relations as a problem to be solved, Mr. Van Buren and Ms. Peabody recognized the inequality and inhumanity of racism. In describing the westward movement, they discussed the problem of manifest destiny and idea of white racial superiority and the immorality of government policies. But only Ms. Peabody commented on the systemic nature of racism in government policies. Mr. Van Buren focused on the moral or tragic rather than political aspects of Native American-white relations and reservation policies. By barely describing conflict in the early colonial period or at times before the late nineteenth century, they didn't provide a framework for the ongoing history of government exploitation or Native American resistance.

The teachers handled lessons on slavery and the Civil Rights Movement in a more balanced way. They gave several examples of how the nation perpetuated inequality through laws and practices during slavery and segregation, noting that whites and the government punished blacks physically and politically. They also noted that blacks didn't just "take it" during slavery and gave real examples of how blacks and whites resisted slavery and segregation, at times working together to defeat racist institutions. The teachers acknowledged aspects of institutional racism and gave examples of black resistance and white assistance to blacks in challenging racism. On the other hand, Mr. Van Buren and Ms. Peabody framed slavery and the Civil Rights Movement as a problem of fulfilling the nation's principles of equality, rather than as a problem of the ongoing legacy of racism. Ms. Hines' remarks about Africans' involvement in the slave trade deflected attention from the nation's role in perpetuating racism; Mr. Van Buren's comments about "feeling great about ourselves except for the Civil Rights Movement" was another example of framing national history in terms of expanding freedom or equality rather than ongoing racism. Both teachers presented slavery and the Civil Rights Movement as part of a larger national narrative in which black segregation was an exception to the nation's expanding legacy of freedom and inequality, suggesting that racism was an isolated or secondary issue in national history, rather than a fundamental flaw embedded in the economic, legal, political and social fabric of national development and contemporary society.

Like the other teachers, Ms. Hines and Mr. Van Buren also did not frame the lessons with students' understandings in mind. In presenting racism as an exception to national development, they reinforced white students' and parents' views and marginalized those of the black community (see Chapters 3 and 4). The teachers rarely challenged white students' views that racism was a moral rather than institutional problem in the past and racial violence occurred primarily during slavery. They minimized or only sporadically affirmed black students' understanding of the legacy and ongoing reality of racism and violence. Mr. Van Buren referred to improvement of race relations in Oakdale, but never talked about segregation or racism in the North and provided no context for analyzing students' contemporary experiences. In presenting racism as a problem to be solved, the teachers provided mixed messages about the harshness of racial conflict and its significance as a major aspect of national development and society.

Teacher Silences during—and Silencing of—Discussions of Racism

None of the teachers provided extended opportunities for student discussion about race and all of the teachers except for Ms. Jensen seemed defensive when discussing most aspects of blacks' historical experiences. Teachers "covered" painful episodes of racism in national history by doing most of the talking and asking fact related questions and they seemed relieved to move on to less emotionally fraught issues. While white and black students at all grade levels commented on the unfairness or immorality of slavery, segregation or the removal of Native Americans to reservations, extended talk about racism rarely occurred. It was if a great pall hung over the classroom when issues of racism in national history arose. This was especially the case in the fifth grade classrooms, where white and black children said little or nothing in response to Ms. Stone's lessons about racial cooperation or Ms. Jensen's lessons about racial violence.

In eighth and eleventh grade classrooms, however, black adolescents took opportunities to comment on and critique lessons about race. The greatest commentary occurred in Mr. Van Buren's eighth grade class and Ms. Peabody's eleventh grade class, those of the more open, critical and student-centered teachers. One day, while teaching about the Progressive Movement of the late nineteenth century, Mr. Van Buren noted that "the Progressive Era was about progress, but it wasn't shared by minorities and women. Blacks in the South were lynched and even though blacks were no longer slaves, the nation turned a blind eye to lynching." The comment provoked audible remarks from black students: "they treated us like dogs," "nobody cared what happened to black people" and "you don't hear about that in the [text] book." Mr. Van Buren didn't respond to the comments; he continued his pre-planned lesson about the various reforms of the era.

During the first lesson of Black History Month, Mr. Van Buren first elicited but then ignored black students' comments. Mr. Van Buren began the lesson by asking students to generate ideas about famous black people they would like to study. Black students' hands shot up. One student said he'd like to study "famous black people in Congress"; others then mentioned Spike Lee, Janet Jackson, black scientists and black cowboys. Mr. Van Buren then commented "we'll look at civil rights leaders, scientists, and business men." Next, Mr. Van Buren asked students to name movies they would like to see. Black students again responded: *Separate but Equal, Color Purple, Roots, Malcolm X, Black Panthers, Ghosts of Mississippi.* Mr. Van Buren did not acknowledge the suggestions but when a white student suggested, *To Kill a Mockingbird,* he responded, "that's a Pulitzer Prize winner." A black male then suggested a film about Medgar Evers, to which Mr. Van Buren responded, "that's discussed in *Eyes on the Prize,* so we'll already see a film about him." Finally, Mr. Van Buren asked students to take out a piece of paper and list one or two things they wanted to learn. He collected the papers, but he never referred to them.

The following day, Mr. Van Buren asked students to turn their attention to the posters of famous black Americans hanging throughout the classroom. He asked each student to select one person and create a drama strip which recorded "the person's early life, beginning career, important events, and the results of their accomplishments." When a black student asked if could do a drama strip on Jesse Jackson, Mr. Van Buren replied:

> Jesse Jackson was religious and supported Louis Farrakhan and the Nation of Islam. But a lot of people saw that as controversial. I don't want to get into that now, because I want to hear from another couple of people about the positive effects that African Americans have made in this culture, American culture, and African American culture.

Although Mr. Van Buren asked for student input into the curriculum and black students enthusiastically obliged, he only acknowledged suggestions that fit into his preconceived ideas about what was significant in black history or what he felt comfortable discussing. He ignored, avoided or criticized most of the black students' suggestions about important historical actors and films and censured some black students' selections of the black Americans they wanted to research. By having asked for and then ignored students' suggestions, he signaled that he really wasn't interested in student input, especially from black students about black history. And by closing down rather than opening up discussion about figures like Jesse Jackson and Louis Farrakhan, he further alienated black students interested in learning more about prominent figures and missed opportunities to discuss their beliefs.

As I reviewed my field notes on Mr. Van Buren's unit on black history, I tallied the number of times that white and black students asked or answered questions or made spontaneous comments. During the three week unit, white students spoke a total of 21 times, not including questions about assignments or presentations of their drama strips. They withdrew from conversations about the significance of black Americans in history and even the more talkative eighth graders rarely responded to questions or made comments. Black students, however, made 88 separate comments about black actors or events in history and many asked questions about actors or events that Mr. Van Buren could not answer. More black eighth graders were engaged when the subject matter turned to black history and their engagement turned into active participation. But Mr. Van Buren's discomfort with controversial black figures or black nationalist perspectives on black history and his limited views on what counted as positive black leadership prevented him from acting on black students' interests and participation.

Several examples of teacher silencing and silence also occurred in Ms. Peabody's eleventh grade class when black students took the lead in answering questions and offering spontaneous comments about racism. For example, when Ms. Peabody mentioned that in the seventeenth century some blacks had come to the colonies as indentured servants rather than as slaves, one black male student wondered aloud—loud enough for all to hear—if "whites had tricked blacks" into thinking that they were coming to the colonies as indentured servants. "Once blacks got here," he said, "I bet the whites made them slaves and never meant to give blacks freedom." The comment prompted another black student to wonder aloud, "how could Europeans act so cruel? If they were Puritans and believed in being pure, how could they have slaves?" A third black student then said:

> did anyone stop to think if whites wouldn't have got lazy and decided they wanted someone else to do their work, that black people wouldn't have had to go through all of this? Why go out and buy all this land knowing that you can't work all this land? That's stupid.

Ms. Peabody did not respond to the black students' comments and continued teaching the lesson as if nothing had been said.

Ms. Peabody similarly ignored black students' comments during a lesson on slavery. When she said that white slave owners beat or whipped blacks who disobeyed orders, three black students gave further examples of white violence: "whites cut off their toes when they tried to escape," one black young woman said. Another noted that "sometimes their hands or legs got cut off" by engaging in dangerous work and a couple of students commented on the fact that "white men raped the women" and "there wasn't nothin' anyone could do about it." Black students also referred to other forms of abuse, such as whites who sold black children to other owners, or whites who tore up the "freedom papers" of blacks who had been emancipated but were returned to slavery. A few days later during a discussion of black participation in the Civil War, one student commented that northern and southern whites feared black participation because blacks might turn their guns on whites. Another commented that whites were pleased about black participation because blacks were sent first into battle to die. Ms. Peabody did not respond to students' comments about racial violence or race relations and once again missed opportunities to affirm black students' knowledge about race relations.

Two weeks later during a discussion about Reconstruction, black students asked questions or contributed comments about the aftermath and long-term effects of slavery. "What happened to blacks when slavery ended," one asked, "when they set slaves free, did they roam around?" Another heard that "a lot of black people trashed their white names and took African names;" a third said that "some owners blackmailed freed slaves and said they owed them money and the black people couldn't leave." The last comment sparked a discussion on contemporary racism among black students. "The law says that no one can be discriminated against, yet whites still don't consider blacks equal or give them the good jobs," one black student commented. Another student said "there's still racism, it's just more subtle now." Other black students concurred and referred to police profiling of black males and the media's portrayal of welfare recipients and drug dealers as black. "Most welfare recipients are white but the media doesn't tell you that," one black student remarked. Once again, Ms. Peabody did nothing to affirm, challenge or contribute to black students' commentary about racism historically or in contemporary society.

Conclusion

The six teachers' interpretations of race and rights in U.S. history provided mixed messages about the importance of the contributions of people of color, the role of white violence as an enduring historic theme, and the expansion of rights throughout the nation's history. All of the teachers included a few social justice oriented lessons related to race and rights: they recognized the exclusionary nature of the Bill of Rights in early national history and discussed how blacks and women had to fight for freedom and rights. They included examples about black resistance to slavery and segregation and Native American resistance to land encroachment and expropriation in the nineteenth century. And most discussed whites' and blacks' participation in the Underground Railroad and Civil Rights Movement, which provided white and black students with examples of interracial cooperation.

Most of the teachers, however, presented mixed messages about the limitations of rights, the extent of institutional racism historically and white people's participation in and benefit from it historically and today. The teachers presented rights as exclusionary in early American history, but subsequently conceptualized rights in positive and optimistic terms which eventually extended to all Americans. And only Ms. Jensen presented racism as a theme endemic throughout the course of national history and society. The other teachers either emphasized racial cooperation or conceptualized racism as tragic yet sporadic problem which became less problematic as the nation developed. Overall, they presented racism as an insignificant, exceptional, immoral or limited problem, rather than as an integral, institutional and enduring aspect of national life and rarely presented white people or Northerners as perpetrators or beneficiaries of racism or violence. They referred to black resistance during slavery, segregation and the Civil Rights Movement but not throughout the course of national history. And they silenced or ignored black adolescents' commentaries about the intentions, motivations, strategies and tactics which whites used to keep black people down.

What effects did the teachers' pedagogies have on the historical explanations and interpretations of the students they taught? In the next chapter, I analyzed how teachers' pedagogies influenced students' historical explanations and interpretations about race and rights. The analyses revealed that even in teacher centered classrooms, the teachers had some effects of children's and adolescents' explanations of historical actors and events. Teachers' pedagogies, however, had minimal effects on the interpretive frameworks or broader narratives through which students filtered teachers' lessons about race and rights in history.

3

THE RACIAL DIVIDE

Differences in White and Black Students' Interpretations of U.S. History

In this chapter, I examined the explanations of historical actors and events and interpretive themes with which students began the school year, focusing on differences in white and black students' explanations and interpretations. I then analyzed their end-of-the-year explanations/ interpretations and compared them to those they had constructed at the beginning of the year (see Appendix C for an explanation of the research methods). The analyses provided evidence about the effects of family/ racialized community discourses and teachers' pedagogies on students' explanations and interpretations of race and rights in U.S. history and contemporary society.

White Students' Pre-Instructional Explanations and Interpretations

Racial Groups

In September, white students depicted Native Americans in terms of tribal or economic organization: Native Americans "lived in teepees" or "had different tribes," fifth graders commonly replied and adolescents gave similar responses: "some lived in longhouses, they fished and grew plants or had different religions." Two adolescents referred to Native Americans as the "first Americans" or "first people here." They described enslavement as a time when "blacks picked cotton, slaves worked for other people or slaves worked without getting paid." They next referred to blacks during segregation of the 1950s, noting that "blacks and whites went to different schools, they couldn't go to the same schools or they had different stuff for blacks and whites." They credited Rosa Parks and Martin Luther King, Jr. for "wanting freedom or rights" or "standing up" for black people and conceptualized the Civil Rights Movement as a movement by and for black freedom or rights. A few adolescents credited desegregation ("everybody can use the same bathrooms") and/ or equality ("whites and blacks are equal today") as the consequences of the Civil Rights Movement. Overall, white students imagined Native Americans as isolated groups existing prior and not contributing to national development; they represented blacks as victims rather than as historical subjects or nation builders except during the Civil Rights Movement.

Conversely, white students described Europeans, European Americans and/or whites positively throughout the course of national history as explorers, discoverers, leaders and inventors. Most described European explorers as having opened up new lands and few identified personally, saying that "we wouldn't be here without them." Fifth and eighth graders uniformly credited Columbus with having discovered America, as did all but two of the eleventh graders. A majority of adolescents described George Washington or Abraham Lincoln in positive terms, while some saw them as having united the country. A few adolescents described the westward movement as a time when "people went west for gold": others saw European immigrants as having contributed to diversity or explaining "where our ancestors came from." They also identified positively with John F. Kennedy, whom they described as a "good or great" President or as a President who "wasn't stuck up" or "helped ordinary people." Overall, white fifth, eighth and eleventh graders constructed Europeans and white Americans as those responsible for having established and developed a nation based on freedom and equality and some identified with white historical actors personally or collectively.

Race Relations

White students infrequently referred to race relations. They rarely named Europeans, whites or Southerners as perpetrators or beneficiaries of racism or as allies of people of color. Two adolescents referred to

Native Americans' assistance to European explorers ("they helped with food" or "showed settlers how to hunt"); none made any references to racial conflict or the depopulation of Native American tribes. In explaining enslavement, only one white eighth grader named whites as slave owners; the other adolescents referred to blacks as unpaid laborers but not to whites as slave traders or owners. A few fifth and eighth graders said that slaves were "treated mean" but didn't say by whom; the one eleventh grader who referred to physical violence—"slaves might get whipped if they didn't do what they were supposed to"—didn't name the perpetrators of violence. Four adolescents referred to whites or Southerners as segregationists who perpetrated or benefited from segregation, i.e. "white people thought they were better than blacks" or "we kept them from doing stuff." None, however, referred to acts of racial violence during segregation or the Civil Rights Movement.

National Development and Identity

White students explained national formation and development in positive and progressive terms. They saw the nation as having expanded rights to marginalized groups and related the outcomes of national growth and democracy to their own identities as Americans. Eighth and eleventh graders explained European settlers as having begun the country and "if it weren't for them, we wouldn't be here." They saw the American Revolution as a time when "they started the country on the road to freedom," the Declaration of Independence as having led to separation from Great Britain, the Constitution as "about freedom, rights or all men are created equal" and the Bill of Rights as "rights to do what we want" (fifth graders) or "gave us our freedom and/or rights" (eighth and eleventh graders). A few adolescents saw the late nineteenth century as an expansive era when "people went west for gold or spread across the country" or "immigrants made our country a melting pot." Others explained World War II and/or dropping the atom bomb as having made the U.S. a world power or as having spread democracy. With the exception of enslavement, segregation and Nixon's resignation, white students explained national formation and development as having promoted economic growth and expanding democracy; with the exception of the Vietnam War, they interpreted the nation's involvement in foreign wars as having contributed to the nation's position as a world power and the spread of democracy abroad.

Overall Themes

After eighth and eleventh graders selected and explained important actors and events, they reviewed their choices to consider what had and hadn't changed over the course of U.S. history. Most reinforced the positive and progressive views of the nation which had emerged in their explanations of individual actors and events. Johanna, a student in Ms. Hines' class, provided a narrative in which Europeans/whites were the primary nation builders, rights for all and discrimination both existed in the past and Americans worked together successfully to dislodge inequality:

> All things changed America in some way. Columbus discovered America; Indians tribes helped us and were here before anybody. Exploration helped with discovery, after settling the colonies they needed amendments because they couldn't have anarchy. The Bill of Rights gave people rights. With the immigrants, if we wouldn't have rights and freedom then when they came to America, they could have just said "take them back."
>
> Suffrage … that gave women rights to express their feelings and opinions. The Civil Rights Movement tied into the Constitution because everybody should have rights. King, Rosa Parks … showed people that it wasn't fair and they stood up for black people and marched … Some people didn't like it but they did what was right. Now things are pretty good and anybody can go to school or sit where they want and get a job.

Andrea, another eleventh grade student in Ms. Peabody's class, had a greater sense of diversity, conflict and bigotry as part of national development, yet still presented a positive and ultimately triumphant national story:

> People from another country coming over and discovering colonies and developed and people learning to live together. Then slaves coming over and you have Indians who own the land and you got people speaking out saying "it's wrong, we're all the same" and you got people who want to make a difference, to be able to live together and help civilization. If you

got people fighting all the time, how is your land gonna develop? Why not come together and help each other out?

Like the founding fathers wanted people to be together and wanted to help people. Same thing with Rosa Parks and Martin Luther King, Tubman, one person speaking out for something and people listening. Here they are with ideas and people are so strung out on their ways they don't want to change, but these people are saying something is wrong with this and you got people coming together. I can't say finally because there's still discrimination today, but just think of how it would be if these people were never born ... Thanks to these people, we have civil rights, the Bill of Rights, there's nothing that says you can't do this because of your color or ethnicity.

Like those of several white adolescents, Johanna's and Andrea's narratives told a progressive tale of national development, where European immigrants settled the land, created a democracy based on freedom and rights and built a world power which supported democracy at home and abroad. Originally excluded from participation, blacks and women stood up for their rights and with minimum conflict or struggle against unnamed adversaries, achieved freedom and equality. Overall, white students constructed positive views of national history and identity, ones in which the nation progressively included greater numbers of people into a democratic society based on ever expanding or equal opportunity and rights.

Black Students' Pre-Instructional Explanations and Interpretatons

Racial Groups

Like white students, black children and adolescents also described Native Americans in terms of tribal organization, i.e. "they lived in different types of houses" or "used all parts of the buffalo." Black adolescents, however, were more likely than white students to refer to Native Americans as the first settlers: "they were the first people here" or "they were here when Columbus came." The majority of black students explained enslavement as a time when "slaves worked hard" or "white people" made them work hard. Several students remarked that they "felt sorry" for slaves, slavery "wasn't right" or "they had to work hard and didn't get paid." Adolescents also discussed black contributions and experiences beyond slavery and the Civil Rights Movement. Some described twentieth-century black migration to the North as a political process where "they moved for greater freedom" or "there was still racism in the North but it was better than the South." Others saw migration in personal terms: "they moved north to give their children a better life" or "this is how my family got to the North." Some adolescents referred to black scientific or technological discoveries, commenting that blacks often received no credit or "whites took credit for black inventions." They also commented on black participation in the Civil War and World War II: "blacks proved they could fight" or "blacks and whites fought together instead of against each other."

Black students expressed pride when describing black leaders or the black people during the Civil Rights Movement. Most commented on Rosa Parks' or Martin Luther King's courage in "not moving for a white man, standing up for black people or ending segregation" and considered them to be role models. On the other hand, adolescents had mixed views towards Malcolm X: some supported his ideas about self-defense while others disagreed with his early views of racial separatism. Most however admired his ability to turn his life around, change his views and/or "like King, fight for our freedom." Some adolescents also explained the Civil Rights Movement as a collective effort: "black people got tired of being pushed around so they did something about it" or "King couldn't have made progress without all the people who supported him and marching. You need both for progress: a strong leader and people behind him."

In describing Europeans/white Americans, black students explained them as nation builders, as those who took credit for others' accomplishments or lied about their accomplishments, and as oppressors and, in rare cases, allies of blacks. Black fifth graders referred to Columbus as an explorer or discoverer but adolescents rarely credited European explorers or Columbus with discovery. Instead, many pointed out that "Indians were here first" or "Columbus was known for discovering America but he didn't or he lied." While all knew that George Washington was the first President, three eleventh graders added that he or Jefferson owned slaves. One eleventh grader called the founding fathers hypocrites because "they preached one thing and did another." The three adolescents who selected European immigration as an important event explained its significance negatively and conflated historical and contemporary images: "immigrants took the opportunities of people already here" or "immigrants brought diseases with them." Black students held uniformly positive views of Abraham Lincoln and John F. Kennedy. They described Lincoln as having "freed the slaves, tried to help blacks or lived up to his promises," although one referred to Lincoln as a "joke: he freed slaves but didn't think they were equal." They thought well of John F. Kennedy, seeing him as a president who "helped black people" or "tried to end segregation."

Race Relations

A few black fifth graders referred to "friendly" Native American-white relations, noting that "Indians and Pilgrims became friends or they had a big dinner with Columbus or Pilgrims." A few adolescents referred to conflict between Native Americans and whites, commenting that Native Americans had to move for "Americans or whites" or "they got kicked off their land." Adolescents also discussed white violence towards blacks. Several referred to beatings and whippings during slavery; others gave more graphic examples. A fifth grader, for example, learned from his grandfather that "some slaves ran away and they'd get dogs to chase them and if they found them, they'd [the dogs] wrestle them to the ground." An eighth grader recounted that "whites whipped slaves if they acted up and didn't get much food and had to pick cotton all day in the hot sun." One eleventh grader heard that "when one person was punished, they all had to watch ... people had their middle toes cut off if they tried to escape." Another lamented, "some slaves ran away and got killed; who knows how many died?"

Black adolescents described segregation as a time when "whites were racist, thought whites were better than blacks, or gave blacks the raggedy stuff." One eleventh grader described segregation as a continuation of slavery:

they freed the slaves but whites were still racist and split up blacks and whites. It was wrong how black people wouldn't get the good water fountains or bathrooms. It's important to know how this happened and how people straightened it out.

Young males especially referred to racial violence or related it to family members' experiences: "you'd get kicked if you drank from the wrong fountain," an eighth grader commented, or "my uncle had to move from the South because some white man was after him," an eleventh grader explained. Adolescents also described King or the Civil Rights Movement in terms of racial conflict: King "stopped the violence" or "made peace between blacks and whites." One eleventh grader explained that

> the Civil Rights Movement was where there was a lot of fighting between the races … America wasn't all goody goody. When the media showed the police with dogs attacking people, it put pressure on the government; it didn't look good."

Black adolescents also critiqued white or mainstream views of black inferiority. Some referred to white views of black inferiority during enslavement or segregation, noting that "whites thought blacks were below them" or "whites didn't think blacks were as smart." In explaining black participation in wars, one young woman commented, "they can't say we didn't do anything for the country." Some gave more critical responses, noting that "whites didn't think blacks could fight" or "whites let blacks fight in the Civil War so they [whites] wouldn't get killed."

National Formation and Identity

Black children and adolescents began the year with tempered and somewhat negative views of the nation's founding and development. Adolescents connected the Declaration of Independence and/or American Revolution with separation or independence, rather than freedom or rights. Half of the black fifth graders and a third of the eighth and eleventh graders associated the Constitution and/or Bill of Rights with freedom or rights, but the majority explained the documents as "rights for some people, not everybody has rights or it didn't apply to black people." Two fifth graders associated the Bill of Rights with arrest or incarceration, i.e. "the police have to read you your rights if you do something wrong." A few eleventh grade young men explained that racism and lack of equal rights was something they dealt with when security guards followed them in a mall and police stopped them for "dwb" (driving while black).

Black students rarely identified personally or collectively with national development. Only occasionally did they use words like "we" or "our" when describing the Declaration of Independence, American Revolution, Constitution, or Bill of Rights. When describing World War II or Vietnam, they didn't express pride in the nation as a world power or as a supporter of democracy; instead, a few critiqued the nation's involvement in wars, suggesting that their original motives might have been "to help people, but they always got something out of it." Black adolescents conceptualized national formation and development with the creation of a nation built on principles that should have been—but weren't—for everyone, and associated national identity with oppression and/or exclusion at home and self-interest in world affairs.

Rather than identifying with a national history or identity based on freedom or rights, black students identified with blacks as a people. Some adolescents used "we" when explaining slavery or segregation and many referred to "we" or "us" in their explanations of civil rights leaders and events, i.e. King "stood up for us" or "didn't let whites walk all over us." Another presented civil rights in harsher terms: "we got sick of being treated like dogs and did something about it." Several commented that King, Parks and/or Malcolm X were role models for blacks, noting that the civil rights leaders' actions enabled today's black youth to have opportunities that they would not have had otherwise or provided lessons for ways to stand up for oneself and challenge racism in contemporary society.

Overall Themes

When reviewing their selections of important actors and events, black adolescents focused on black struggles for freedom and equality. They presented a portrait of a nation that oppressed rather than included marginalized groups and more often exploited rather than spread democracy. They were of two minds about racism and rights in contemporary society, however. A few adolescents believed that blacks had equal rights, as evidenced by the end of segregation and right to vote. As Tanya, an eighth grader explained, surely but slowly blacks started rising and were able to do more as time progressed. Now we're able to live together, go to the same schools, we're innocent until proven guilty and we're not guilty because of the color of our skin.

A majority of black adolescents, however, had more pessimistic views of race and rights in the past and present. They attributed racial conflict and struggle, rather than progressive nationalism, as the means for inclusion, saw racism as ongoing and institutional rather than exceptional or individual and identified with blacks as a people rather than the nation as an entity devoted to democracy. In assessing change and continuity, Tina, a student in Ms. Hines' class, spoke primarily of the continuity of racism and her cynicism towards government as a lever for democratic change:

> In the past, blacks were fighting for what we believed and today blacks still struggle for equality. There is still racism today; it's something you have to live with. The government drove the Indians off their land and they're fighting to get it back. The government controls everything but doesn't do much to help anybody. Like in Bosnia, they're not going over to help them; they're going to get something out of it.

Dwayne, a student in Ms. Peabody's eleventh grade class, also focused on racism when thinking about change and continuity and critiqued the black community's drift away from racial solidarity, as well as the mainstream media's underestimation of protest. At the same time, he had a more positive view than Tina about the ability of the black community to create positive change:

> Racism is still here. Rodney King, he resisted arrest but they didn't have to beat him like that … African Americans fought for a while to get freedom and equality for the right to vote. Women had to fight to vote too … After the Civil Rights Movement, we began to stop to fight for freedom and began to turn on our race …
>
> The Million Man March showed we can do the same thing, fight for our freedom and rights, come together as a people. I went with my uncle, dad and cousin … they tried to say there weren't a million there, but I got off the bus and saw all these black men. It was peace and harmony and I thought there might be violence but there wasn't any. Like the media

says we're all violent. It showed me that we could come together as one and make our streets safe.

Differences in White and Black Students' Pre-instructional Interpretive Frameworks

White and black students began the year with different interpretive frameworks about the role of race and rights in national formation, development, identity and society. White students constructed a nation in which Europeans and white Americans positively created and transformed a nation based on economic growth and opportunity and democracy and rights for all—with few exceptions—at home and abroad. They saw Native Americans as a pre-national neutral presence and blacks as victims without violence of nameless oppressors until the Civil Rights Movement. For most, they interpreted contemporary society and national identity in terms of the ubiquity of rights and racism as a thing of the past.

Black students interpreted the nation as having been created by and for European/white Americans who enjoyed economic and political rights from which people of color in the United States and people around the world were excluded. They interpreted white historical actors and whites as a group as nation builders *and* oppressors. More black than white students credited Native Americans as having been the continent's first settlers and they interpreted blacks as nation builders *and* victims of white oppression. Most black adolescents interpreted national history, society and identity in terms of whites having had greater rights than others and racism as continuing to mark the nation's history and contemporary society.

Effects of Pedagogies on Students' Historical and Contemporary Explanations and Interpretations

Although white and black students began their history classes with different and conflicting interpretations of race and rights, their teachers had only a vague knowledge of students' understandings. The teachers generally believed that white students needed to learn more about black experiences and all students needed to learn more about the contributions of all racial groups; the cooperative, conflict-ridden or problematic nature of race relations; and the initial struggle for and eventual acquisition of equal rights. The teachers presented a range of content and activities related to these themes, but with the exception of Ms. Jensen, they embedded these within interpretive frameworks which aligned more closely with white than black students' understandings. The teachers also rarely engaged students in instructional activities which either enabled teachers to learn about students' views or which scaffolded students' thinking towards concepts of history and society rooted in social justice.

Nonetheless, the teachers' pedagogies had some effects both on white and black students' historical explanations, especially in cases where teachers spent a considerable amount of class time on a specific historical actor or event. In some cases, instruction changed white and black students' pre-instructional explanations in similar ways; in other cases, it changed one but not the other group's views and in other instances, it shaped both groups' views but in different ways. In the next section is a description and analysis of how instruction affected white and black students' historical and contemporary explanations of racial groups, race relations and individual rights, as well as an explanation of when and why instruction shaped and did not shape children's and adolescents' explanations and interpretations.

Effects of Pedagogy: White Students

Racial Groups

Fifth, eighth, and eleventh grade students reflected their teachers' instruction about differences among Native American tribes and the majority incorporated ideas about Native Americans as the first inhabitants. They also reiterated instruction about Native American assistance to early settlers and a few eleventh graders mentioned the government's placement of Native Americans on reservations, which they thought "wasn't fair or right." In explaining enslavement, about half of the white students named whites or Southerners as slave traders or owners and several referred to slaves having been "treated mean" or the institution as "unfair" or "not right." A few adolescents also picked up on instruction about "owners or whites" having whipped or beaten slaves. Similarly, several students named "whites" or "Southern whites" as those who "didn't let black people use the same bathrooms or go to the same schools" during segregation. In September, they referred to separate facilities but not to the individuals or institutions responsible for segregation.

White students also incorporated many of their teachers' lessons on the Civil Rights Movement. Most elaborated on their pre-instructional knowledge of Parks and King as major players and role models and several reflected instruction about leaders and events having brought rights or equality to all people, rather than just blacks. An eighth grader, for example, echoed a common description of King "making everybody equal." A few students referred to whites as having thought of themselves as superior to blacks, while others referenced the Movement's multiracial nature: "it showed," an eleventh grader in Ms. Hines class said, "that blacks and whites could fight together for what they think is right." Many students referred to desegregation and/or equal rights as the Movement's consequences:

King stood up for people's rights and everyone was listening. His main purpose was for everyone to be treated equal and not the color of your skin determine where you sat or ate. He got rights for everybody and now anyone can go to school and places together and not have to be separate.

In describing Europeans or white Americans, white students generally accepted their teachers' instruction about the significance of whites in national history. They reflected instruction and elaborated on their earlier views of European explorers, settlers and colonists as important contributors to national formation and, like their teachers, credited them with having started and developed a democratic nation. But unlike their teachers, students did not refer to the founders' limitations as having supported rights only for elite white men. Instead, they incorporated instruction into their prior models of leaders as extenders of freedom and democracy. Instruction changed their views only of Columbus and other explorers, whom they described as explorers rather than discoverers.

A few eighth and several eleventh graders also reiterated their teachers' instruction about the significance of late nineteenth-century European immigration. Typical comments constructed immigrants as those who "worked in the factories and farms and helped the country with industry" or "made this country what it is today." A few saw a connection between immigration a century ago and their own lives: "that's how we find out about our ancestors and where they come from." Several echoed instruction about immigrants' contribution to the nation's diversity: "all these people immigrated into the United States and that is how we became known as the melting pot," an eleventh grader asserted.

Race Relations

As a result of instruction, most students commented on differences among Native American tribal communities in the early colonial period; a few also referred to Native American assistance to white settlers. A few adolescents selected as significant Native American-white relations in the nineteenth century. One young man in Ms. Peabody's class explained that the government "wiped out the Indians," three adolescents referred to the government's removal of Native Americans to reservations, and one said that as a result of the reservation policy, Native Americans "now get benefits from the government." In terms of Native Americans' contributions and experiences in national formation and development, white students, like their teachers, had limited knowledge of Native Americans and they rarely appeared as part of their national narratives.

Although students in September were aware of whites or Southerners as slave owners and segregationists, only a handful actually named them or said they "treated slaves mean." At the end of the year, however, many students referred to whites as slave owners and commented on the "mean" treatment of the enslaved. A few students also referred to beatings or whippings, even in the classrooms of teachers who emphasized racial cooperation. Even limited instruction about the role of racial violence during slavery seemed to prompt white students to name whites as oppressors of enslaved blacks.

White students were less likely, however, to refer to racial violence during segregation and the Civil Rights Movement, even in classrooms in which teachers talked about white resistance or violence. None of the fifth graders in Ms. Jensen's class, for example, referred directly to the death threats King had received or the bombing of his Atlanta home, as they had read about in class. After having read the story, Ms. Jensen asked the children to write a letter to King's children. White children rarely mentioned racial tensions or even the assassination of King. Instead some included condolences about his death, but didn't make references to violence surrounding King's life and death:

> I wanted to know how you felt after your father's birthday passed. I know it was hard when you father passed away. Just know that we will always keep your father's dream in our hearts. I'm glad you father's dream came true. (Ashley)

> I wrote this letter because I wanted to know how did you feel after your father died? So how are you doing? What have you been doing? What has your wife been doing? (James)

Adolescents described segregation in terms of whites having superior resources, facilities and attitude and/or as having "treated blacks mean," rather than in terms of physical threats or violence. Several also altered their views of the Civil Rights Movement as a result of instruction. In September, white students saw the Movement as "for, by, and about blacks"; by May, many emphasized its multiracial character and effects. "White and black people marched and/or gave speeches," students remarked at the end of the year, and several said that King wanted "freedom or rights for everybody" or "he was important for everybody being equal." They also reflected instruction in explaining the Movement as having brought about "rights for everybody" or as "King helped everybody get their rights." In May, about half of the eighth and eleventh graders referred to the multiracial nature or effects of the Civil Rights Movement, whereas none had done so in September.

National Development and Identity

As a result of repeated instruction about the limitations of democracy in the eighteenth century, fifth graders in both classrooms changed their pre-instruction explanations of the Bill of Rights from "people can do what they want" to "rights for rich white men only." At the same time, the children still interpreted other early national actors, events or documents in terms of freedom and rights. Some transposed their earlier instruction about the Bill of Rights onto the Declaration of Independence, Constitution or founding fathers, stating they "gave us our rights" or "let people do what they want." At the end of the year, white children incorporated their teachers' mixed messages of the early republic's freedoms and limitations by having ascribed limitations to the Bill of Rights yet having equated national formation overall with freedom and rights.

Adolescents, on the other hand, were not influenced by their teachers' mixed messages about freedom and rights in the early republic. Despite some instruction about the limits of democracy in early America, they interpreted the Bill of Rights and other early national symbols in terms of freedom, rights and the establishment of government. They reiterated instruction about the Constitution as having created order through government, and ignored instruction about the limited applicability of the Bill of Rights by defining it as "giving freedom and rights" or "the rights that all Americans have." They also reflected instruction about the Civil War as having "kept the nation together," the Depression as a time when "Americans stuck together" and World War II as having made the nation a "world power" or "democracy for the whole world." One of the few times they expressed criticism of national policies was during the Vietnam War, which they interpreted as a "mistake" or "we shouldn't have been there." With a few exceptions, white adolescents interpreted national formation and development as a progressive advance towards greater democracy at home and abroad. And they continued to identify positively with a nation that they associated with freedom and rights for all.

Overall Themes

In describing what had and had not changed over the course of national history, most eighth and eleventh graders incorporated instruction which reinforced their pre-instructional views about the progressive nature of national formation and development and positive view of national identity. They acknowledged the immorality of racism and had a deeper understanding of blacks' and women's struggles to gain freedom and rights. Although their beliefs about the extent of racism in contemporary society varied, most still had an optimistic view of national history and identity.

Johanna, for example, in September represented change in national history as a positive and almost effortless extension of rights to women, immigrants and blacks, which all enjoyed today. Her interpretation at the end of the year reflected a greater sense of struggle but no less sense of progress or belief in a national identity based on democracy:

> Our country was put together by motivated people and people who wanted to change, to better themselves and our country. That's why they left Europe; they wanted to find a better land. They didn't want to live by other people's rules; they wanted to establish their own way of life. They [colonists] were fed up with taxes in Europe; they wanted freedom for their own religion and speech and didn't want to answer to a king. The Constitution was about rights and regulations and they felt they could be more fair and productive with freedom and rights.
>
> Slaves didn't like being slaves so they rebelled; if this hadn't happened then things still might be that way. They didn't want slavery so they changed it. Women didn't want to be put down because they were women and wanted the right to vote. So they went out and made a change. The immigrants came over ... if it wasn't for them, we wouldn't have factories and different cultures. And civil rights ... we fought for everybody to have rights.
>
> Everything made a step forward: during World War I we thought we were better than everyone else and nothing could happen to us and then we mess up and go into the Depression and learn from our mistakes. World War II, we won the war and got respect and helped with democracy in other countries, and then they started the UN and another step forward for peace. And Vietnam, they thought it was a step forward. The fight for equal rights: women wanted to vote and blacks wanted to vote and be able to do things without people being mean to them and that's how it is now.

Johanna's narrative revealed lessons about the contributions of Native Americans, the Constitution and immigrants to national development and "everybody's" contribution to the Civil Rights Movement. She also incorporated Ms. Hines' progressive views of national development, power and the spread of democracy at home and abroad. She did not, however, reflect lessons about the limitations of rights in the Bill of Rights, represented the oppression of women and blacks as exceptions to equal rights and blacks' and women's struggles as relatively simple and conflict free. Overall, Johanna tended to incorporate aspects of Ms. Hines' instruction which contributed to her pre-existing image of the nation as based on democratic rights and rule and discounted or simply did not include the exclusionary, conflictual or violence-ridden parts of the nation's past.

Andrea provided another example of students' inclinations to accept instructional content and themes which extended but did not fundamentally alter their pre-instructional views. As a student in Ms. Peabody's class, Andrea began and ended the year with a greater sense of racial struggle and conflict than did Johanna. But like Johanna, she viewed national formation, development and identity as rooted in principles and initial experiences of freedom and rights.

> Back in the 1700s, a lot of people came from Europe and wanted to create their own country. They didn't want other people telling them what to do, so they had a revolution and started the country and came up with laws and rights for people. But people were segregated too. The Indians helped when the settlers came but the government took their land and put them on reservations. And blacks were slaves and worked hard and were abused. But we're always going to have racist people. People in the North thought it was wrong and wanted to keep the Union together. The Civil War freed the slaves and kept the country together, so things were more together as a nation.
>
> Then the immigrants came and didn't have rights but they worked hard and spoke up for themselves and worked their way up to the rights of Americans. Then we won World War II and became powerful but we still had to solve the problem of segregation. Blacks and whites marched and had speeches and got more rights for blacks and others. Today, you still have segregation; that's the way people are brought up. But people can do more now. You have black judges and governors and black people can apply for jobs even though if a black and a white person applied for a job, the white person probably would get it.

Like Johanna, Andrea imagined the nation as having originated from a motivated people who wanted freedom and democracy. She incorporated lessons about Native Americans and blacks as having contributed to and been victimized by the nation. She also reiterated ideas about the rise of immigrants and national power, the need to "solve the problem" of segregation, and the multiracial nature of the Civil Rights Movement. Like Ms. Peabody, Andrea also vacillated in her views of the nature of racism: at times she discussed it as a characteristic of individuals; at other times, she discussed its institutional nature.

In terms of rights and racism in contemporary society, about half of the white adolescents believed that all people had rights and racism was nonexistent or related to individual discrimination. Two white students continued to see racism as a problem in contemporary society and blamed white people or the government. Jim, a student in Ms. Hines class said:

> In America, there has always been segregation because you are always going to have racist people and you are always going to have war. People think that just because they are in office, they can do whatever they want. How many presidents actually kept their promises? In the past, African Americans wanted to own a farm or business and today, homeless people want a home. Southerners split up African American families; today the government might take homeless people's families. You'll always have segregation; that's the way things are set up.

About one-quarter of the white adolescents thought that even though racism no longer existed, black people express anger towards whites. One student used the example of history teaching during Black History Month, which he resented and held black students responsible for racial tensions that emerged. He also presented historical actors or events as having belonged to either white people's or black people's histories, rather than all Americans' history:

> When black history comes around, it's nothing but problems. Black kids are mean to the white kids, like it was us who were the slave owners. During Black History Month, we have to do all these reports and many white kids don't want to write about a famous black guy that gave all of the black people rights. Or when we had to watch the riots and stuff on TV, it just gets us riled up. We don't get upset when we see the Constitution or the Declaration of Independence. But when civil rights come around, blacks get angry. They feel like they were tortured. That was in the past.

Blacks think it affects them but it doesn't. There shouldn't be slavery but I don't think whites should be looked down upon.

Effects of Pedagogy: Black Students

Racial Groups

Like white children and adolescents, black students reflected instruction about the variations in Native American tribes and none referred to "friendly" relations with settlers. A greater number of adolescents in May credited Native Americans as having been the first Americans and discredited Columbus as having discovered America. Adolescents also incorporated instruction about the African slave trade and a few confused European explorers to the Americas with European slave traders. Many elaborated on their pre-instructional explanations about the particularities and harshness of enslavement: "blacks had to work as slaves for whites and whites used chains around their necks and feet so they couldn't escape." Others learned about the significance of slave rebellions: "slaves were tired of being slaves so they rebelled or ran away."

Several eleventh graders credited blacks for participating in the Civil War, which they had learned about from watching the movie *Glory*. The eighth and eleventh grade teachers didn't discuss black migration to the North and only Ms. Hines mentioned black participation in World War II. A few black adolescents, however, included these events as significant. They explained migration as having enabled "blacks to be free in the North" or "even though there was racism in the North, it was better than in the South." Others had learned from home or the media that blacks had served as pilots or boat captains in World War II or that "blacks fought in World War II but they segregated them in separate armies" or "they didn't think they were as good as whites, but they showed they could fight and help out." Even though the teachers did not provide a continual record of black experiences or accomplishments, some adolescents incorporated information they had learned about outside school.

In describing the Civil Rights Movement, black students elaborated on some aspects of teachers' instruction about leaders' actions and the Movement's effects. They continued to explain King, Parks and Malcolm

X as they had in September as leaders and role models for blacks today. A few connected the outcomes of the Montgomery bus boycotts to their own lives. One eleventh grader, for example, explained that

> they had a bus boycott and all the black people didn't use the buses and the white bus drivers didn't get money so they let black people ride the buses ... and sit where they wanted, in the front or the back. And it was good that they did that because now we can sit wherever we want on the bus ...
>
> One time when I was on the bus with my grandmother and I went up the back, she said, 'why you sitting up the back, come down here and sit up front. People didn't fight for you to be sittingin the back.' And my mom always is saying something how Martin or Malcolm didn't fight for us to be acting like a fool.

Similarly, black adolescents used instruction to elaborate on their pre-instructional views of the Civil Rights Movement: black leaders and/or people fought for and/or achieved rights for blacks. Overall, black students incorporated content from instruction which affirmed and amplified, rather than altered, their pre-existing understandings of the period and tended to ignore information which contradicted their knowledge of the Movement as for, by and about blacks.

In explaining whites' experiences, black students tended to incorporate content which debunked whites as heroes and not include or interpret differently lessons which credited whites for discovery or nation building. More students in May than September explained Columbus or European explorers as not having discovered America and some commented Columbus "lied" about discovery. Two adolescents pointed out that "he was trying to discover something else and ended up in the wrong spot." They saw the founding fathers as having established a new nation, but not one built on freedom and rights. The few adolescents who selected European immigration explained it in the same negative light about job competition with "real" Americans which they or others had in September. One eleventh grader stated that "millions of immigrants came over and by doing this, the Americans here were placed into a big hole ... millions of people competing for jobs and things ..."

The two leaders that most black students viewed positively in September and May were Abraham Lincoln and John F. Kennedy.

Most credited Lincoln with emancipation, although a couple of eleventh graders said that Lincoln cared more about national unity than emancipation and one referred to Lincoln as a hypocrite for having thought of blacks as inferior to whites. None of the black students represented negative views of Kennedy. Instead, they referred to him as a President who "wasn't prejudiced," "helped black people," or "didn't like what was going on with segregation."

Race Relations

As a result of instruction, a few black children changed their explanations of Native American-white relations. In September three children referred to "friendly" relations between Native Americans and whites, but by May, none had. Two in Ms. Jensen's class had learned that "men came and took the Native Americans' land" and one learned about Native American poverty in contemporary society: "they're off by the side of the road selling pots and stuff." Adolescents used instruction to elaborate on tribal differences and a few who hadn't referred to nineteenth-century conflict in September did so in May, stating that "the government kicked them off their land" or "they stuck them on some land nobody wanted." An eleventh grader in Ms. Peabody's class learned that "Indians showed them how to plant and live on the land and they ended up putting them off of their own land and using their ideas against them."

Instruction also amplified children's and adolescents' views of racial violence and attitudes. Fifth graders picked up on instruction about physical violence towards enslaved people and blacks during segregation. In letters to King's children in response to the bombing of King's home, black fifth graders in Ms. Jensen's class—unlike the white students—referenced racial violence:

> I wanted to know how you felt when your father got those bad phone calls. I would be sad because no one should be gunned down because he helped black and white be friends. Because of him, I have a white friend and I don't have to worry about the black and white stuff. (Desiree)

> I wonder if you are feeling better about your dad. I wonder if you got any bad phone calls saying "I want to kill you." I wonder if you miss your house that got burned down. (Marcus)

Adolescents also referred to racial violence, abuse or hierarchy. Many referred to physical abuse, intimidation and death throughout the course of history, learning that "millions died on the way over from Africa, overseers used the whip to keep blacks in line, and bounty hunters chased blacks to the North and might kill them if they had to." They also noted that "[black] people went to the North for jobs, there was racism in the North, it just wasn't as bad as in the South." Adolescents also referred to white superiority in beliefs, employment and public facilities and some described segregation as a time when "whites walked all over blacks" or "blacks got the lower part of the deal."

None of the black fifth graders in Ms. Stone's class or eighth graders in Mr. Bloch's class reiterated lessons about racial cooperation during slavery. A majority of adolescents did not refer to racial cooperation during the Civil Rights Movement. Most explained the civil rights leaders as role models for blacks and considered the consequences of the Movement as having "got more freedom or rights for blacks" or "ended the fighting" or "brought peace" between whites and blacks. Only a handful of students referred to non-blacks' participation in the Civil Rights Movement or effects of the Movement on non-blacks.

A few adolescents, however, incorporated instruction about racial cooperation. A few eighth and eleventh graders expressed surprise that whites participated in the Underground Railroad or gratitude towards Lincoln for his part in emancipation. A handful of children and adolescents also reflected instruction about the multi-racial nature or effects of the Civil Rights Movement. They explained King as having "wanted rights for everybody" or "brought everybody together." A few also explained the Civil Rights Movement as having "whites and blacks in marches together, been for blacks, Hispanics, Asian Americans, everybody or made everyone equal."

National Development and Identity

The fifth grade teachers' instruction about the limitations of the Bill of Rights influenced black children's explanations. They explained the Bill of Rights in May as "rights for rich white men," rather than as they had in September, i.e. "rights to do what you want" or "not all people have rights." But they did not reiterate lessons about other early national symbols as having represented the principles of freedom and rights. Rather, black students learned that the Constitution was about "rules" or "regulations" for the new nation, rather than freedom or rights. They explained the Declaration of Independence and American Revolution as about "separation from England" or "people wanted their own country" and the founding fathers as having "started the country" or "got the government going." Although their teachers taught about early nationalism as having laid the foundation for equal rights, black students did not associate the period with freedom or rights.

Adolescents also did not reflect instruction about national unity or the positive growth of the nation's power internationally. They explained the Civil War in terms of emancipation but rarely in terms of national unity. Adolescents in Mr. Bloch's and Ms. Hines' classes learned that the Depression "was a time when everybody was poor," rather than a time when "people stuck together." One student in Ms. Hines' class connected the problems of the Depression on nineteenth-century European immigration, a connection which Ms. Hines never made: "by all these people immigrating at one time, this brought on the Great Depression of 1930. All those people coming to America at one time took the jobs of the Americans. Thus there was no money, no jobs, people going homeless, starvation."

Overall Themes

When asked to discuss change and continuity at the end of the year, most black adolescents focused on the progress of blacks' experiences and varied in their views of contemporary black life. Four adolescents thought like Tanya, who began and ended the year with beliefs that blacks "slowly but surely started rising" to the stage where they have equality today. They used instruction to provide more detailed or elaborated views of black struggle and progress than they had at the beginning of the year:

> At first, black people were slaves but when they got their freedom some of them became their businessmen. Millions went North because it was better up North and wanted a better life for their children … During civil rights, there was a struggle for equal rights and people like Martin

Luther King, Jr. and Rosa Parks helped us with marches and boycotts. And today, we can go to the same schools, and have the same freedom of speech and can't get thrown in jail because of the color of our skin.

Dwayne, however, represented a majority view by discussing both racial progress and racism and constructing a collective racial, rather than national, identity:

> It started in Europe where royalty tried to oppress people so they started their own country. But then they started oppressing people. Like *Animal Farm*, the pigs were being oppressed but as soon as they got into power, they did the same things … Then there was trading slaves; bringing them from Africa to America because they needed people to work on plantations. There's been progress but these things shouldn't have happened in the first place … It's not as bad, we don't have slavery now. It's not necessary to put people in slavery to build a nation. I think the whole thing is about struggle; they had to struggle for a war of independence, they had to struggle to be a superpower. In the Civil Right Movement, we had to fight, be patient for progress to happen. You have to sacrifice to make a better life. Today blacks still struggle for equality. There is still racism today; it's something you have to live with.

Tina, a student in Ms. Hines' class, represented a third and less prevalent perspective expressed by black youth. She didn't reflect instruction about racial cooperation or race as a problem to be solved. Instead, she reiterated themes about racism as an embedded and ongoing part of national history and identity as she had in September. She ignored instruction about the nation as an entity which extended democracy at home or abroad and held onto the cynicism towards government she had had in September:

> The theme of black history is the same [over time]. Fighting for what you believe in, struggle, equality, even now, it's like a struggle for equality. You know, like first the slave rebellions, then moving to the North and the Civil Rights Movement. It's always been a struggle. Today, you still have racism. I go into a store and get looked at in a different way, and I'm not waited on but it's something you have to live with.
>
> I see the government still controls everything. Like after the Civil War, blacks were free but they still kept them down with lynchings and

laws that they couldn't vote. And World War II … the U.S. wins the war and then starts taking over in Vietnam and stuff. They go to other countries when there's something in it for them … and pretend it's about helping the other country.

In addition to beliefs about the continuity of racism and cynicism towards government, some black students also critiqued how textbooks and teachers misrepresented race relations. Joseph, a student in Ms. Peabody's class, expressed a lack of credibility in history textbooks, and of the broader mainstream culture's view of black history and culture. When asked if or how well the schools presented diverse racial groups or viewpoints in history, Joseph's comments echoed the opinions of a majority of black adolescents:

> The textbook isn't going to tell you about all the hangings they did to black people. They'll tell you they had slaves and it's not good to have slaves. They don't tell you how they raped the women and stuff. They just tell you what they want you to know.
>
> I'm basically learning about white people's history. Textbooks should go into detail when they talk about blacks, just like they do with whites. I think they should talk about all races and don't beat around the bush. They should tell how white people treated black people and what they did to the women … People who wrote the Constitution were hypocrites because they preached one thing and did another. Black people thought we helped build this country. We did the majority of work. You couldn't vote; you just worked. You couldn't have anything: it was taxation without representation.

Conclusion

White and black students began and ended the year with different explanations and interpretations about the role of race and rights in national formation and development. They also constructed different ideas about the meaning and significance of a national identity. White students began the year with concepts of Europeans or white Americans as heroes and nation builders throughout the course of national history, Native Americans and blacks appeared intermittently primarily as victims and occasionally as isolated and exotic people (Native

Americans) or civil rights leaders (blacks). They held unwavering beliefs in the ubiquity of rights and saw the oppression of people of color or women as exceptions to the nation's legacy of expanding democracy and power. They equated national history and contemporary society with democratic rule at home and abroad and a majority believed that equality existed in contemporary society. The few who believed that racism still existed saw it as individual, rather than institutional, in nature.

Black students began the year with a different interpretive framework. They thought of Europeans or white Americans as nation builders and oppressors of blacks and other people of color, blacks as historical subjects as well as victims who struggled against oppression throughout national history, and Native Americans as having had "friendly"or conflict-riddent relations with whites or the government. A large majority of black adolescents and some children saw racism and exclusion from democratic principles or promises as ongoing, institutional, and inevitable aspects of national history and identity.

Teachers' pedagogies tended to amplify rather than alter students' pre-instructional explanations and interpretations and had greater effects on students' explanations of individual actors and events than it had on students' underlying interpretive frameworks. As a result of instruction, white children recognized the limitations of the Bill of Rights, some children and adolescents recognized Native Americans' contributions to national development and others acknowledged the government's expropriation of Native American lands. Some named whites as enslavers and/or segregators and described the multiracial character and effects of the Civil Rights Movement. Instruction also had some limited effects on black children's explanations/interpretations. Many recognized that the Bill of Rights did not include women and people of color besides blacks, while some learned about Native American-white/government violence and conflict and a few saw whites as occassional allies as well as oppresors of blacks.

While the teachers' pedagogies reshaped students' explanations of some historical actors and events, pedagogy had very little effect on students' overall interpretive frameworks. Even in classrooms where teachers' interpretations conflicted with or contradicted those of their students, students generally continued to interpret race and rights in May as they had in September. For example, even though all of the teachers discussed the limitations of rights at the beginning of national history, white adolescents held onto their pre-instructional ideas, associating unlimited rights with national formation and development. And black students in May constructed race relations in terms of violence and conflict and rights as more exclusionary than inclusive, even in classrooms where teachers taught about racial cooperation and the progressive expansion of rights. Overall, most of the white teachers and students constructed ideas or narratives of national formation, development and identity in positive and progressive terms. They constructed explanations and themes about diverse social groups having gained greater or equal freedom, rights over time and racial inequality as a thing of the past or a matter of individual prejudice. Black students, on the other hand, at the end of the year still constructed the nation in less positive terms, as one marked by racial violence and conflict which continued to exclude marginalized social groups.

In the next chapter, I've analyzed the differences in white and black parents' interpretations of U.S. history, stories they've told their children about relatives' historical experiences and their views of the purposes of school history. I've also examined the differences in white and black adolescents' presentations of national history and contemporary society in school and community-wide settings. The differences highlighted the congruence between white parents' views of history and those presented at school, the dissonance between black parents' interpretations and school knowledge, and the agency of some black adolescents to present publicly the interpretations of history and society which their teachers silenced or marginalized in history classes.

4

BEYOND THE CLASSROOM DOOR

Differences in Adolescents' and Adults' Interpretations of History and Society in Home and Community Settings

Differences in white and black students' interpretive frameworks originated in family/community discourses and experiences about race and rights, historically and today. The differences were manifested in parents' interpretations of U.S. history, the stories about historical and contemporary experiences related to race and rights which family members discussed at home, as well as in the movies, documentaries and other media children and/or their parents watched or listened to. The differences also were represented in single-race and mixed raced school-wide and community settings, where black and white adolescents presented their interpretations of U.S. history and contemporary society, as well as their views about the purposes and perspectives of history taught in the schools.

White Parents

Interpretations of National History and Society

In selecting and explaining important historical actors and events, white parents conceived of racial groups and race relations within the dominant interpretive framework and, like their children, most were less critical of national history and, society than many of the teachers. They saw European explorers as significant because "this is where our ancestors came from and they were out looking for better worlds" and early presidents and founding fathers as having "started the nation and got us on the road to democracy." They uniformly praised Lincoln for having ended slavery and uniting the nation and Kennedy as a president "for ordinary people." They described late nineteenth-century European immigration positively as having built the nation through "their sweat and tears," as one parent remarked or as having "made America a melting pot." Nixon was the only white person that the parents criticized for "lying, cheating and making Americans lose faith in government."

Like their children, the parents referred to blacks only during slavery, segregation and the Civil Rights Movement. They saw blacks as victims of slavery and segregation. They conceptualized the Civil Rights Movement as a time when black people stood up for and achieved desegregation and equal rights. Although all of the white parents commented that slavery and segregation were wrong, "un-American," or "immoral," few named Southerners as slave owners or segregators, only two referred to "racial tensions" in the North during their lifetimes and none referred directly to racial violence or whites' beliefs in white superiority during slavery, segregation or contemporary society.

In addition, four parents compared the struggles of blacks after enslavement to those of European immigrants. As one parent explained, "A couple of years after the slaves were freed, more immigrants came over and then it wasn't only black Americans that didn't have equal rights. It was lots of immigrants who were forced to be poor and hungry." Others held more latent negative views of blacks, as evidenced by their lack of mobility. "Most immigrants started out with nothing, not even the language, but eventually moved up the economic ladder one generation at a time," one parent remarked. Another similarly noted that "immigrants worked hard so that their children would have a better life ... they sacrificed for their children and kept them in school and off the streets."

Several parents selected and explained Native Americans as having lived off of the land or as having "helped settlers/us to survive." A few also discussed conflict and war between Native Americans and the government and referred to the immorality of moving Native Americans to reservations. One parent, however, gave a more critical response by naming white Americans' treatment of Native Americans as genocide:

Our ancestors came to this country when the Indians were already here and forced them out of the areas that they lived in. They put them on reservations. I don't see that as being a good thing. Our ancestors forced the Indians from their homelands and that was one of the first genocides of our country.

White parents also interpreted the role of rights in national formation, development and identity through the same interpretive framework as had the teachers. Several described the American Revolution as a time when colonists "fought for what they thought was right, declared independence and didn't let England tell them what they were going to do with their towns." Others identified personally with the colonists: "our ancestors left other countries because they did not have freedom of religion" or "this was a time when we gained our independence from England and became a separate country." All of the parents selected the Constitution and the Bill of Rights as important documents and interpreted them as having laid the foundation for the nation's laws and for individual rights. Two of the 12 parents also described the documents' limitations: "blacks, women and others didn't have rights and had to struggle to get them," one parent replied.

They explained the Civil War as having united the nation and freed the slaves, U.S. participation in World War II as having "saved the world from Hitler" and many also exhibited pride in the nation's emergence as a world power. They credited the nation as having granted equality to blacks as a consequence of the Civil Rights Movement. Like their children, the only time that they were critical of U.S. policy was in relation to the dropping of the atomic bomb and the Vietnam War. Some parents saw the bomb as having contributed to the ending of the war and the growth of American power; others thought it opened up the nuclear age and the arms race. Most interpreted the Vietnam War as a mistake and some spoke of friends or relatives who returned from Vietnam with emotional problems or did not come back at all. One father joked that the Vietnam War was in "full swing when I was getting out of high school and that was the one lottery I won. My number came up 362 and I didn't have to go."

When asked about the themes that structured national history, white parents detailed primarily positive aspects. They imagined the nation as a positive conglomeration of racial and ethnic groups who eventually "became part of the American dream." Most also believed that although equal rights did not exist in the past, the Bill of Rights laid the foundation for the equality that now applied to all Americans. On the other hand, three of the 12 parents conceived of the nation or government in a negative light, and referred to the recurrence of war or unchecked power of big business or government. As one parent explained:

> War is the one thing that goes from the beginning of U.S. history to now. It's the number one business of the whole world. Without that, there wouldn't be much business going on. The number one thing we've learned from our history is that war pays. Pays somebody. When we're not at war, we have people selling guns to people that want to make war. Americans are governed by the car and building, selling, and repairing them. But war might be a bigger business than the automobile trade.

Perspectives on School History

When comparing the history they learned in school with that which their children experienced, most parents believed their children's courses were more inclusive racially and saw this as a positive development. "If you're educated about other cultures, then you may not be so quick in the future to disregard them," one mother said. Many parents saw the lessons on Native American cultures as teaching young people "how hard it was for people to survive"; others commented that Native American history contained valuable lessons about the negative effects of government: "It showed kids that back then, you didn't have to work so hard to pay the government and not pay yourself." Another said, "If Native Americans had greater access to guns, it would have been more difficult for Americans to commit genocide."

White parents also thought it was important for their children to learn about black history. They mentioned slavery and the Civil Rights Movement as important events. They saw slavery as significant in explaining racial segregation in the past and showing "man's inhumanity to man" and the Civil Rights Movement as an example of how blacks struggled to gain their rights. Some parents saw the Civil Rights and Women's Suffrage Movements as positive examples of how people struggled to attain their rights; others saw them as cautionary tales: young people could learn from these examples that their rights to free speech or to bear arms might be threatened and they needed to watch the government to ensure that the government didn't take away their rights.

At the same time, about one-third of the parents thought that Oakdale teachers spent too much time on "minority" history. As one parent expressed it:

> I never knew who Martin Luther King, Jr. was until I was out of high school. But my kids now are 13 and 11 and that's all they hear. That's ok but I think it may be a bit overboard. Not to say it is not important, but it cuts into other things, like our own presidents who had probably more impact on our society today.

When asked what the schools should teach that they were not currently teaching, several parents wanted schools to teach how government worked so that their children will "appreciate living in a free country" and/or understand the power and limits of government. Several talked about the importance of rights in contemporary society and that children needed to learn that "freedom was a hard won right" or "it wouldn't be America unless everyone had rights." Two believed that learning about rights was significant so that "no one can take advantage of you." Two also referred to inequality in contemporary society, or in the words of one parent: "more people of different races and sexes need to have more power." Two others thought that if their children learned more about the limits of governmental power, their children's generation would be less vulnerable to encroachment on individual rights. When asked to elaborate, one father feared government intervention in the right to own guns; one mother referred positively to local or state referenda where citizens limited the government's ability to tax people.

Overall, white parents, like their children, thought only of Europeans and white Americans as nation builders, portrayed blacks as victims and one-time freedom fighters, and Native Americans first as survivors and later as victims of government policies. They never mentioned whites (other than Southerners) as perpetrators or beneficiaries of racism and 80 percent believed that blacks had achieved equal rights today. Most identified the early nation with freedom and rights and described national development positively as the nation acquired international power and granted equality to blacks. Although there was some variation in white parents' beliefs in the extent of inequality today, most believed in a national history and identity marked by freedom, rights and expanding opportunity. Generally satisfied with the history taught in their children's schools, their major suggestion for improvement involved more instruction on the operation and limitations of government.

History At Home

In sharing with children their or other relatives' experiences, white parents most often told stories of the hardship that they or their children's grandparents had endured. They did this so that their children would appreciate how well off they were in comparison to former generations. Most told stories of financial difficulties, such as having to share limited resources with several siblings or having to walk miles to go to school. In relating events of the 1960s, several parents discussed "the hippie movement" and anti-war protests in which a few parents had participated. A few also discussed current events. In discussing Operation Desert Storm and the invasion of Iraq in the 1990s, one parent discussed the significance of history and the nation's place in the world:

> We talked about the stuff with Iraq because that can affect our lives. I've got a niece that's joining the service and my daughter should be aware because her cousin is going. Kids need to be aware of what the people and the country have been through. Even going back to the Civil War, we fought for changes.

In discussing what the schools should teach children about national history, a couple of parents mentioned ways to lessen violence in contemporary society and turned to history as an example from which young people can learn:

> Young people need to learn that there are ways of going around the violence. A lot of history shows a lot of violence. You need to be able to figure out alternatives to violence. We need to learn from our past mistakes. I guess that's what history is about, problem solving.
> *Interviewer:* When you say there's been violence in history, what do you mean?

Parent: All the wars we were in; millions of people died ... There have to be better ways to solve problems besides war.

When asked about family stories related to history they learned about at home, white eleventh graders had learned about their grandfathers' military service in World War II and their grandmothers' work in factories to support their families and the war effort. Grandparents also told stories of tough economic times: many walked miles to get to school, others worked many hours in addition to attending school, some had no electricity, and a few noted simply that "it was hard to survive." Some eleventh graders had fathers or uncles who had gone to Vietnam and all recounted negative or frightening experiences. One young woman's father had worked as an airplane mechanic in Vietnam and "his nerves were shot" from having worried continually about the safety of the planes. Another young man's father told him that his jeep had broken down in enemy territory and the father thought that he would die that night. Parents also talked about John F. Kennedy as a "really good President who tried to get things done," their "hippie days" when they rode motorcycles or watched Elvis Presley and the Beatles on television.

About half of the eleventh graders also said that their parents mentioned the immorality of segregation in the South or the moral leadership of Martin Luther King, Jr., although they did not have extended discussions about race in national history or society. Two adolescents noted that their parents had talked about race relations in Oakdale in the 1960s and 1970s, a time when tensions were high. One young man had heard how whites and blacks "yelled at each other when someone walked by the classroom"; another learned that "when riots broke out and whites and blacks were fighting, they had to close the school."

Although there was some variation in white parents' interpretations of race and rights in national history and contemporary society, they interpreted the nation's past and present in ways which were similar to those of most of the teachers. They construed whites as nation builders and people of color sporadically as victims throughout history and saw national formation, development and identity as a positive and progressive movement towards expanding rights which resulted in equality in contemporary society. Most parents were less critical of race relations than the teachers who taught about race as a problem to be solved but at least they did not think about slavery or segregation in terms of racial cooperation. Like the teachers and white students, white parents believed in a national past and present marked by rights, equality and opportunity.

Black Parents

Interpretations of National History and Society

When asked to select and explain important historical events, all of the black parents included the slave trade for explaining "how Africans came to America" and for having revealed "the real story" of American race relations. They found the Constitution's significance in having established the political and legal foundation of the new nation and the Bill of Rights' as having granted "rights for white men or white people" historically. Several also noted that rights "are not applied equally to all races today." They selected the Civil War and the Emancipation Proclamation for having freed African Americans from bondage, but also noted that it did not release freed blacks from servitude. Several selected government removal of Native Americans to reservations, commenting that whites wanted the land. One father commented that the policy demonstrated "how far the government was willing to go" to accommodate "people's greed for land."

Most parents then turned to segregation in the South, which subordinated blacks to whites and included physical and psychological abuse. They also noted that segregation was national rather than regional in scope and although life in the North was better than in the South, blacks faced discrimination everywhere in America. Black parents explained World War II's significance as having stopped Hitler or fascism and as having made the United States a world power. But they also commented on government-supported racism during World War II in the segregation of black servicemen. They described the Civil Rights Movement as a time when blacks worked together to show that that "racism can be beaten back" and life can get better when "we work together for change." They explained Parks, King, and Malcolm X as having provided positive role models for black people by having stood up for their beliefs and risked their lives. They wanted black youth to learn about these and other black figures so that they would not take for granted the opportunities that they had. Black parents believed that the Vietnam War was senseless and the nation never should have been involved. Some spoke of relatives who had served in the military, which they found to be "as racist as the rest of America," in the words of one father's uncle.

Unlike white parents, black parents saw national formation and development as having been based on white supremacy and black oppression. They presented enslaved and segregated blacks and Native Americans as victims, except during the Civil Rights Movement, when black leaders and ordinary black people fought as a people for rights. They saw rights historically and in contemporary society as a significant part of white privilege, identified with blacks as a people rather than the nation and conceptualized a national identity based on white power and privilege.

Perspectives on School History

Although black parents thought that U.S. history taught to their children was more racially inclusive and honest about racism than the history that they had learned in school, they still believed that teachers and textbooks underrepresented the contributions and experiences of blacks and other people of color. A few parents said it was important for children to know about Native Americans' struggles historically and today to maintain their livelihoods and culture. Others noted that national policies had caused greater damage to the populations and cultural heritage of Native Americans than to those of Africans or African Americans. As one parent commented, "at least black people held onto their culture; they took everything from them [Native Americans]."

Several black parents also remarked that the schools taught about blacks only during slavery and the Civil Rights Movement. "I'm tired of having my kids hear about slavery," one parent proclaimed. Another noted the negative effects of youth culture on black adolescents' views and was disappointed that the schools did little to provide positive images of blacks and realistic images of national history:

The black history that our kids get from the media is more of the rap variety, rather than the real history, which is positive, like what black people have done years and centuries ago. They should go back to Africa and know about some great black people in ancient history. Then work our way into U.S. history.

And there's still not enough in the history books. Like Frederick Douglass, you see his picture, but you only find about this much. If you want to really learn, you've got to research it yourself. I think it would be an advantage to all kids to get real knowledge of how the country is. Things weren't so pretty like they make it in the textbook.

A few parents noted that Europeans or whites still received credit in history textbooks for the accomplishments or discoveries of others:

My daughter learned that Columbus discovered America. But there are other people who did this, but you only hear about Columbus and there are people who dispute it, so I try to tell her to listen to all of it and make up her own mind.

Black parents also alluded to the absence of discourse on white oppression. One parent suggested that "most teachers and textbooks don't really teach about how whites kept blacks down after slavery. They had Jim Crow and race riots but you don't learn about those things at school." Two others referred to teachers or texts as having downplayed or whitewashed the role of white violence and believed that older children ought to learn about racial conflict. One parent noted that it was impossible to understand contemporary society and race relations today without a grounding in the history of white intimidation. "They used the whip, the government, anything they had to keep us back," one parent explained.

Several parents also talked about civil rights leaders as role models who "helped black people get to where we are right now." One parent commented, "to me, it still isn't equal but we are here. You can't make us go away now that we're here." Two parents also expressed disappointment or disdain over the depiction of the Civil Rights Movement in schools and the mainstream media, representations that one parent described as "something about peace and love," rather than about "hate and beatings and killings." One parent referred to "10 great Negroes of American history" approach that schools took to teaching history, while another critiqued the reification of King to the exclusion of other black leaders with more radical messages. When his daughter asked him about the lack of information on black people in history textbooks, one father remarked:

> In the history books, you see just a little in the book on people like Frederick Douglass, as great as he was. You see his picture, the man with the beard, but you only find out so much. If you want to learn what really happened in this country, you've got to go research it yourself.

History at Home

Because of the limited and distorted information on black experiences presented in schools, about half of the black parents said they discussed black experiences at home, often in the context of the family having watched a movie, documentary or newscast. After watching *Mississippi Burning,* one parent told her children about growing up in Mississippi and how the son of a white family for whom she worked almost attacked her:

> We tell our kids this to make them aware, that things aren't straight yet, you've got to make the best of your situation. All parents want their kids to take advantage of what's there, and there was racism and there is always going to be racism, and you just make the best of the situation.

Several parents or grandparents watched and discussed with their children or grandchildren documentaries and films on Martin Luther King, Jr., Malcolm X, and other prominent blacks. Some celebrated Kwanzaa with their children and two parents listened with their children to black talk radio programs. Others talked about racism that they or their parents had witnessed in the North, including cross burnings in the yards of black families and physical attacks by white men on black men.

Three of the 12 parents supplemented their children's education in more formal ways. One father sent his children to an African American academy on Saturdays for tutoring and enrichment on black issues. "I want my kids to know black history, to know where you came from and give you a sense of pride and know that black people have done things and you can do things besides play basketball and football." Another parent enrolled her daughter in a Saturday program at a black history museum and used flashcards of famous African Americans to teach her daughter about the ways that blacks contributed to national and scientific development. Another mother took her children to bookstores with strong collections on black history and education, and she and her son read and discussed the books that they had bought. Two encouraged their adolescent children to participate in NAACP activities organized for high school students, seeing the organization as a positive force for black youth cultural and social development.

Half of the parents also commented positively on the 1995 Million Man March. Two of the fathers had taken their sons to the march, while the other parents watched it on television with their children. One parent summed up the march's significance in the following way:

> To me, the Million Man March represented a positive thing to see that black men are into a bit more than sex, be-bopping, hanging out. We are positive, we do love our kids, and all of us aren't what they want to say, we don't deserve our kids. There are so many single black parents and there are a lot of positive black men. It was a positive thing coming together to do something positive. I tell my son that people are going to be tough on him because he's black so you got to get your program together. You can do it, it can be done.

While the parents of black fifth and eighth graders filled in the gaps about black accomplishments and experiences that the schools had failed to teach, eleventh graders reported that the black history they learned about at home "opened my eyes to how black people really lived," as one young man said. Some eleventh graders reported having learned of relatives who had moved from the North to the South in the 1920s and of the relatively greater freedom accorded to blacks in the North. Some family members informed young people about black inventors and one student said that he was surprised to learn that "it wasn't all white folks. I didn't know that black folks invented anything until my grandmother told me." Another grandmother told her granddaughter that during slavery, some masters left money or possessions to slaves, which explained how some black people, including those in her family, had accumulated some wealth. Others heard stories of relatives who owned businesses, cars, and land.

By far, however, the greatest number of stories passed down between generations related to racism. Several students had uncles, fathers, or grandfathers who had lived in the South and had been physically threatened or beaten by whites, which caused their families to migrate north. Living in the North was no guarantee of physical safety however. Adolescent boys particularly heard stories about black men in the North who had been intimidated or beaten by whites. Other young men heard stories about racism in World War II or Vietnam. One young man had a great uncle in Vietnam who received taunts from white servicemen: "niggers shouldn't be over here fighting the war," the young man's relative related. The great uncle agreed with those taunting him and replied, "I didn't want to fight this war for you."

All of the black eleventh graders had heard stories about the Civil Rights Movement, Rosa Parks and Martin Luther King, Jr. and some had relatives who referred to Malcolm X. Parents, aunts and uncles and grandparents discussed with pride their involvement in civil rights protests or in having seen Parks or King. They also presented the figures as role models for youth. Several adolescents had heard stories of Rosa Parks, which ended in a moral lesson to "always stand up for what is right if you feel someone has done you an injustice." Several had parents or grandparents who commonly referred to King or Malcolm X when instructing young people on social or moral behavior. One young woman commented,

> when your parents tell you something, it always has Martin Luther King's or Malcolm X's name in it. 'He wouldn't want you to do that because he fought for so many things for you.' And now it's like we're taking it for granted.

A few young men had heard stories about the Black Panthers, a group who "stood up for all the black people living in the ghetto. They wanted black people to come together," one young man had learned, "so if anything happened to a black person, all the black people would be together."

Differences in White and Black Family Members' Interpretations

Race-related differences in white adults' interpretations of race and rights in national history and contemporary life not only paralleled those of their children and adolescents, they also were congruent with the frameworks of national history taught in schools. Although some white parents presented critical perspectives on the government's treatment of Native Americans and involvement in Vietnam, they generally presented positive perspectives on national formation and development. They saw national history as having originated in a people's quest for self-government and in the creation of inalienable rights eventually enjoyed by all Americans. Like their children, white parents and other relatives thought of Europeans and white Americans as nation builders and people of color primarily as victims. They associated violence in national history with war rather than race relations and rarely named whites as agents or beneficiaries of racial violence or superiority (Terkel, 2005). In Oakdale, white adults' interpretations of national history, society and identity conformed with those presented by most of the history teachers and textbooks which their children encountered in school. For them and white Americans in general (Rosenzweig & Thelen, 1998), discussions of historical actors or events served mainly as a backdrop for illuminating family member experiences and for adults in Oakdale particularly, stories about family or national history often provided lessons about their children's financial security relative to those of former generations.

Black parents, however, constructed much more critical interpretations of national history, society and identity than those presented by white parents and teachers and textbooks in schools. The parents in Oakdale, like blacks nationally (Gwaltney, 1993), saw the nation's formation and development as based on whites' physical and psychological subordination of blacks and believed racism continued to be the most significant issues defining national identity and facing contemporary society. Like their children, black parents conceived of the concept of rights as perennially exclusive rather than progressively expansive. Even though black parents interpreted the Civil War as having freed enslaved blacks, they still saw the nation as having used law and custom to segregate blacks and dispossess Native Americans. They interpreted the Civil Rights Movement in terms of black agency and pride and people like King and Parks as having provided important role models for black youth. All of the black parents saw racism in contemporary society as embedded in the nation's history and identity, something that their children had to learn to challenge and accommodate.

Like white parents, black parents and relatives discussed family members' and others' experiences to enable their children to understand how far they had come compared to black people of prior generations. Unlike white parents, however, black parents discussed history at home critically and as a response to racism. Family stories about the experiences of relatives or other blacks was a means to teach children about the contributions of blacks to national history and society, as well as about the role and legacy of racism, something parents believed that their children would not learn at school. History in black homes was more than a mechanism of situating black children within the course of black experiences; it was a mean to prepare them for the harshness of racism and violence in contemporary society (Epstein, 1998; Rosenzweig & Thelen, 1998).

Adolescents' Interpretations of History and Society

School-Wide Settings

During the course of the study, black graduate students and I attended a number of school and community events in which white and black adolescents initiated and/or participated. The purpose was to evaluate how adolescents interpreted historical and civic oriented topics outside the classroom and assess if or how young people's racial identities shaped their interpretations. One event which illustrated some black adolescents' views towards black experiences in national history was the annual Black History Month assemblies sponsored by the Black Student Association (BSA) of Oakdale High School. An hour and a half in duration, the assemblies took place in February in the high school auditorium and all of Oakdale's middle and high school students and faculty were required to attend.

Each year, the assembly began as one or more black students took center stage to sing *Lift Every Voice and Sing*, the black national anthem. One year, an adult guest speaker signaled its significance by referring to the author's accomplishments and the song's message to black youth:

> This was written in honor of Abraham Lincoln's birthday by James Weldon Johnson, a graduate of Atlanta University who had worked as a teacher, lawyer, songwriter and diplomat. It is the song of your quest for dignity, your quest for empowerment, the quest to control your own destiny, that you create a world that is not violent and insane.

Afterwards, a BSA member recited poems by well known black writers, including Langston Hughes' "Freedom Train", Maya Angelou's "Still I Rise", and Countee Cullen's "I Wear the Mask." Next, a student or a parent read an original poem about the struggle for civil rights, ending black-on-black violence, and empowering all young people to fulfill their potential. Two or more dance or musical performances followed and each assembly ended with an inspirational speaker who discussed the significance of education for all youth.

One year, BSA members presented a skit written by an eleventh grader. The student said he wrote it because he wanted "everybody to know what slavery was really like, how they killed and maimed people and treated us like dogs." The play opened with a 105 year-old woman about to tell her great grandchildren "the *real* story of how slaves were treated." The scene then switched to an antebellum Southern plantation, where an enslaved husband and wife hauled sacks of cotton. Suddenly, the slave master and white overseer appeared and the master grabbed the woman by the shoulders. The enslaved man punched the slave owner in the face and ran from the pursing overseer. The master then dragged the woman into the "big house." The husband surreptitiously slipped back to the plantation to learn that the master had raped his wife, who was pregnant. The master suddenly appeared and shot and killed the husband. In the last scene of the skit, the 105 year old narrator commented to her kin:

> This is a story of how African Americans were held in bondage. They didn't have a place to go in society. They had a voice, but could not be heard. We were looked upon as not being people. We were counted as three-fifths of a person. Look at today's times and how things have

changed because of the fight that African Americans have fought throughout the years. We have the opportunity to be lawyers, musicians, brain surgeons, producers, landowners, storeowners, and full people. The sky is the limit and a good education will take you there.

During each assembly, white students entered the auditorium subdued and with voices lowered. Black students, however, became animated as they entered the auditorium, waving furiously to friends. All students and faculty stood up during the singing of the black national anthem and black students sang along with those on stage. After each performance, white students clapped politely for the obligatory amount of time; black students cheered, stamped their feet, and responded to the calls of their classmates on the stage. Teachers, for the most part, tried to keep order and broke up pairs of students, black and white, who continued to chatter throughout the program. One black student, upon entering the auditorium, muttered to a peer, "this is *our* day."

When we interviewed BSA members about the black history assemblies, they said that they initiated them so that "our history and culture wouldn't be lost." They also sponsored a Kwanzaa celebration, which black students voluntarily attended. Several BSA members commented that the schools in Oakdale in general, and social studies classes in particular, did not address issues related to black history, black culture or "issues in the black community now." Some thought that their teachers did not discuss black history "except for slavery and Martin Luther King" because they did not know much about the historical experiences of blacks. Others thought the teachers didn't care, didn't think black history was important, or were afraid to teach about the "real deal about race relations in America."

Although a minority of black students were involved in working with the Black Student Association, the students' efforts and interpretations spoke to the gap in the education the students had received through the official curriculum and social studies classes in particular and the self-education they engaged in through voluntary means. Because teachers and textbooks ignored the frameworks on history and society that black youth learned about at home and through other black-oriented institutions, some black youth publicly displayed and disseminated critical black perspectives on history and society. The displays included not just the inclusion of black culture and biography; young people also addressed the role of violence in race relations and the range of alternatives which black people had created to respond to racism and marginalization.

Mixed Race Settings

In addition to attending school wide events, I also participated in youth-oriented community activities. For three years, I served as a judge for the Oakdale Optimist Club's annual essay-speech contest on civic responsibility for middle school students. In addition to promoting civic responsibility and concern for community, the Club's mission was to "talk health, happiness and prosperity to every person you meet." Its leadership and membership were evenly divided between white and black adults and the atmosphere at Club meetings was respectful. Family members attended the breakfast at which middle school students delivered their speeches on topics like making a difference in the community, visions of responsible citizenship and a fair society, etc.

The speeches of the 20 white middle school students whom I judged were organized around individual concepts of opportunity, mobility and citizenship. They highlighted the importance of getting a good education and participating in sports; the need to stay away from drugs and attend college so that they could become a professional and support a family; the importance of cleaning up the earth so that their children would live in a healthy environment; and the significance of treating others with respect. Several commented on the importance of having faith in God and being a good citizen. As one young man noted, "I always obey the laws of my country. I'm proud to be a citizen and ask what I can do for my country." Another extolled the virtue of "staying committed and anticipating the best. I already have responsibilities to do homework and take care of pets and this will make me a responsible citizen when I grow up." The adolescents organized their civic identities around concepts of professional opportunities and civic responsibilities as individual actors.

Black students also discussed their responsibilities to become professionals and responsible citizens, but did so by discussing the obstacles they faced, the means they had to address those obstacles and the responsibilities they had to give back to the black community. Black middle school students discussed staying away from drugs, alcohol, sex, teen pregnancy, and gangs, as well as standing up for "what's right and letting people know when they are wrong." Several praised their mothers for "raising me right" and saw the significance of getting a good education and becoming a professional so that they could be responsible family and community members. They discussed the importance of education and becoming a professional and compared black educational attainment to fulfilling Dr. King's dream that "everyone can be great because everyone can serve." Two students also referred to studying black history in college: "Blacks need to know the history of black people not taught in books and we need to do something with this." As future citizens, the students discussed working to end racial profiling, white-on-black violence and black-on-black violence. Like white middle school students, black students imagined a present and future marked by individual accomplishment and citizenship involvement. Unlike white students, black students also exhibited a sense of communal responsibility to the black community (Cooks & Epstein, 2000).

Black Settings

In all-black settings or for all-black audiences, black high school students presented a range of critical interpretations of race and rights in national history and society. One group of high schoolers published and circulated at Oakdale High School an underground newsletter entitled *The Amistad*. According to the masthead, *The Amistad* was sponsored by "Force Productions, an alliance of 16 African Americans all under the age of 21 who are trying to get up and do something in their community." In the first volume, the editors explained that the publication's purpose was to promote "unity and self-determination among young people, to educate and inform our young brothas and sistas so we together can combine our efforts to fight 'Mr. Charlie' [i.e. white people] and his racism." The newsletter contained poems and prose that eschewed black-on-black violence and criticized those who sold out to "the man" and/or were ignorant of black culture. It also included the Black Panther Party's philosophy, listed the names of imprisoned and murdered Black Panthers, and called for black nationalism and self-determination. In both issues, the editors explained to their readers the meaning and significance of the term "black power":

> Black Power meant the amassing of black people of political, economic and social power, the power necessary to deal effectively with the problems they had faced as a powerless people regulated to a life of poverty in an affluent society. It also called on black people to reject social values which were responsible for their status in the United States and to replace them with an ideology which embraced dignity, pride and blackness. Black people would purge the patterns programmed by a society built on the alleged ethical, moral, and intellectual superiority of the white man. Black power is often equated with violence; the presumption was that white people were justified in getting what they wanted through the use of violence, but African Americans had to pursue their objectives only through appeals to moral conscience.

When I asked the young men why they started the newsletter, they talked about the need for black youth to educate themselves in a society which mis-educated them. "White America doesn't want us to know about how how blacks fought back," one editor commented. The other young man spoke of how "white America imprisoned" black men physically and psychologically and how gun control laws came about in the 1960s as a result of black men using guns to protect their community. The young men thought it was important for black youth to understand how black people historically educated and empowered themselves, as well as how they defended the black community against all forms of racism. The young men learned about black nationalism and other forms of empowerment from one of the young men's older brother who majored in black studies in college. The high school students saw it as part of their responsibility as "responsible black men" to educate other black youth about black history.

Black adolescents in Oakdale also represented their views of history and society formally through NAACP youth activities. For three years, I served as a judge for Oakdale's NAACP ACT-SO (Afro-American Cultural, Technical and Scientific Olympics) oratory contest. The 24 students whom I judged read speeches based on the works of Malcolm X, Martin Luther King, Jesse Jackson, Maya Angelou and other well known activists and artists. Each year, a few students wrote and presented their own speeches. The original essays implored other young people to know their history and end the "mis-education of the Negro," reject black-on-black violence and the prison system, stand up for themselves and other blacks, and support black self-determination. One young man named Derrick articulated his position forcefully:

> We first need to realize that 'the system' was not created for us. When the Declaration of Independence was created, it said, 'we hold these truths to be self evident," but it wasn't talking about us. Remember, we were only three-fifths of a man! ... The foundations of this country are shaking. We as African Americans have been placed in a prison called America. The guards, also known as the United States government, made a mistake by overstuffing the prison ... . What we are doing is venting our anger on each other. We need to turn our anger out on the oppressor because he is the one who keeps us locked down ...
>
> This revolution that I speak about needs to begin intellectually. For hundreds of years, African Americans have been mis-educated about their history, culture and folkways. All we ever learn about is slavery and the Civil Rights Movement and all of the incidents in which we received beatings. We never hear about black militants who were for the educating and empowering of African Americans to move us into our desired position in society.

Another Oakdale student wrote an essay that reflected the tensions she had experienced as a native born Nigerian who had moved to the United States when she was 10 years old and settled in Oakdale. Upset about the images that black youth held about Africa, Imani wrote "Why We Need African Education in America":

> You ask me why I feel it is important to have African education in America. Many of our people don't understand that black people came from Africa. Many feel that because they are born in America, they are not part of Africa. But what they don't realize is that our roots rest in Africa and can be traced back and forth. I cannot blame black people in America for not knowing anything about where they came from because African people have been portrayed and betrayed for many years in negative ways in commercials, television and *National Geographic*. The majority of my generation is afraid to accept the fact that even though

they are born in America, they are African people. Their ignorance remains because they are afraid of not being accepted into the society that discriminates against them.

Since we are not taught about our African roots, we must try to educate people about themselves. We can depend on ourselves and rely on our community for a better education. Having an African education, we can be more exposed to our leaders in early ages, as we are exposed to other ethnic leaders in American history books. Not only black people can benefit from African history but other ethnic groups too. It will give us self-discipline, motivation and knowledge to help us look beyond money and drugs. Each of us can benefit from an African education if society is willing to pay more attention to the ethnic and cultural viewpoints of students and provide them with skills that could help them become productive citizens.

Imani's and Derrick's essays represented critical responses to history education in schools and the broader culture. Derrick used the nation's historic promise of equality to illustrate its hypocracy in enslaving and imprisoning blacks historically and today. He blamed the schools for mis-educating blacks about black experiences and white racism and implored black Americans to stop turning against each other in violence. He, like other young men who talked about turning black-on-black violence into self-defense, saw white racial violence as an enduring issue and black militancy as a viable solution. Imani similarly saw mainstream American education as having mis-educated black youth and teaching African history as a means to enable black youth to develop pride and discipline. She discussed the value of learning about African history and other global areas for all youth and called upon the black community to provide the education and skills to produce proud and responsible citizens. Within the contexts of black sponsored events, youth like Imani and Derrick felt safe to present critical and alternative perspectives on mainstream interpretations of history, as well as a range of solutions that black people have proposed to achieve respect and equality in society.

The critical views of history and society that black adolescents had constructed, as well as their solutions to racism and responsibility to the black community, extended beyond Oakdale. For two years, I accompanied a handful of black adolescents from Oakdale to the

McDonald's Corporation annual luncheon entitled "Black History Makers of Tomorrow." The luncheon hosted all eleventh graders in the greater Detroit area who wrote an essay on "How I Plan to Make an Impact on Black History." Each year, the judges selected five regional winners who came from a range of urban and suburban high schools and socioeconomic levels and the winners read their essays at the annual luncheon. None of the Oakdale students were among the winners, but the essays read at the annual luncheon mirrored the themes that Oakdale adolescents had produced.

Essay winners from throughout the metropolitan area read speeches in which they planned to become professionals and use their professional standing to improve the lives of black people. Although the young people's career aspirations ranged from medicine to architecture to microbiology, all wrote of their desire to work with the black community. One student from a Detroit public high school wrote about becoming an architect or urban planner to "turn the city's empty lots and burned out buildings into parks and playgrounds, provide help to the poor and … reestablish pride in the city." Others talked about becoming doctors and lawyers and "returning to the black community to serve our people." One young man described his dream as a black history maker to go to medical school and come back to his neighborhood and start a health clinic and health classes for youth. A few described their plans to become teachers or professors so they could "pass on our people's history and culture to future generations."

Several students also referred to the lack of black history taught in schools or to the schools' misrepresentation of black history. One student from a wealthy suburb began his essay by noting that the contributions of blacks had been ignored in school history books. Another commented that history books rarely had more than one paragraph on blacks and much of that reported "falsehoods." Others mentioned that they learned about black history at home rather than at school or had read about black history on their own. One young woman planned to become a Black Studies professor to pass on the legacy of black history. She wanted to start an Institute of Black Studies and write a United States history textbook that treated black history comprehensively. Her purpose, she said, was to enable "all Americans to learn about black achievement and blacks to learn about their hidden history and culture."

Students also described the lessons they had learned about the significance of education in general and history in particular to the black community. One young woman acknowledged that it was the struggles of her ancestors that had afforded her and her peers the opportunities to go to school and become professionals. Another young woman planned to teach her own children about black history so that it wouldn't be lost and believed that black youth would be less self-destructive if they learned about their history. Another young woman from Detroit also mentioned teaching her children about the struggles of ancestors so that her children can fulfill their potential. Young people "needn't be Martin Luther King, Jr. to make an impact on black history," she commented, and she cited the thousands who stood behind King. "If it were not for those who boycotted the buses," she remarked, "we still would go straight to the back."

The students also critiqued the mainstream media for circulating negative black stereotypes. They singled out television news media specifically for providing negative images of black youth, but believed they could overcome negative images by becoming positive role models. One student chastised her peers for neglecting to build a contemporary movement for black civil rights. "Too many of us complain about what the white man has done to us, rather than focus on what the black man or woman can do for us," she said. She called on youth to portray the determination of earlier eras and provide new leaders with fresh ideas. Overall, the students asserted that "black success in a white world" was filled with obstacles, but each demonstrated the determination to become a "black history maker" by becoming well educated and giving back to their community.

Conclusion

In homes and community settings, white and black adolescents and adults in Oakdale had the freedom to represent their knowledge and beliefs about national history, contemporary society, the teaching of history in school and civic identity and responsibility. White adolescents and adults reflected interpretations largely congruent with those presented in history classrooms, constructing mostly positive and progressive narratives of national development and contemporary society and ignoring or marginalizing the contributions of people of color, the restriction of rights and the role of racial violence. A majority believed that racism was a thing of the past and people today either received equal rights or discrimination was the result of individuals. They equated national identity with freedom and equal rights and citizenship with individual accomplishment and obligation and viewed public education as the means to individual advancement and fulfillment. In Oakdale, white adolescents and adults generally were satisfied with history taught in the schools and rarely sought extra-curricular activities to supplement or present their views.

Black adolescents and adults sought out the freedom afforded at home and in voluntary associations to present alternative views of history, society, school knowledge and civic and national identity. From family, peers, personal experiences and black oriented media, black adolescents and adults described the institutionalism of racism in national history and society—including the absence of black contributions and role of white violence in school history—as well as the philosophies and practices of blacks in response to racism. They conceptualized rights in history and society as perennially exclusive rather than progressively inclusive and associated the national identity with a lack of freedom and rights for people of color. Black youth and adults saw education and citizenship as an individual *and* collective responsibility to challenge racism for the benefit of the black community as a whole. Barely addressed in history classrooms, some youth and adults turned to alternative educational texts and venues to learn about and present the range of responses to racism that blacks had developed over time, including the need for black self-defense, self-determination and other forms of black nationalism.

5

RE-ENVISIONING THE RACIAL DIVIDE

Teaching and Learning History Across Differences

White and black children and adolescents in Oakdale entered and exited U.S. history classrooms with conflicting concepts of race and rights. Developed from their experiences and interactions with family members and other trusted adults, as well as from peers, mainstream and popular media and their experiences as members of privileged and marginalized racial groups, the differences shaped their overall interpretations of U.S. history, school knowledge, national identity and civic responsibility. White students' interpretations of history and society were largely congruent with those presented in history classrooms and white children and adolescents affiliated with national and civic identities grounded in ideas of individual rights and equality. Black children and adolescents encountered in-classroom interpretations of U.S. history and civic/national identities that contradicted those which they had learned about at home and through the community. Consequently, black adolescents, like adults in Oakdale, learned to distrust the historical knowledge taught in schools and turned to family, community members and black oriented texts and venues to teach themselves and others about blacks' contributions and experiences. They affiliated with a civic identity tied to a sense of responsibility to the black community, and associated contemporary society and national identity with racism and inequality.

Most of the teachers presented nationalist or participatory democratic interpretations of U.S. history and citizenship. Although they believed in incorporating diverse racial groups' contributions and experiences into the history curriculum as a means to broaden students' appreciation for diversity, their practices belied their beliefs. Most teachers presented racial groups' experiences only intermittently, having discussed Native Americans only during pre-colonial and colonial history and the late nineteenth century and blacks during enslavement, segregation and the Civil Rights Movement. Some masked the history of racism by focusing on racial cooperation, while others trivialized the history of race relations as one among many "problems" that the nation needed to and had solved. Only Ms. Jensen related racism historically to racism in contemporary society and all but Ms. Jensen presented rights and democratic practices as having extended over time, resulting in equality today. Like history teachers elsewhere (Almarza, 2001; Lewis, 2003; Sleeter, 2005; Wills, 1994, 1996) Oakdale teachers were not equipped or willing to present the pervasive nature of racism and the exclusionary character of rights as major themes throughout U.S. history and contemporary society. Because the teachers taught about racism and limitations of rights intermittently as exceptions to the nation's progressive development, they provided mixed messages about the extent of inequality in national life and did little to challenge the racial divide in students' historical interpretations.

The teachers seemed even less willing to engage students in conversations about racism, did not address black students' class comments about race relations and white violence or manipulation, and ignored or were ignorant of white and black students' emotionally laden comments about "the other group's" historical experiences. They did not prepare white students to confront the history of racism honestly or non-defensively and rarely addressed black students' concerns about racism throughout the course of national history. Even when the teachers emphasized restrictions on individual rights in the eighteenth century, they elicit discussions or provided classroom activities which reinforced concepts of exclusion. When students raised questions about the unfairness of racial abuse or the limited nature of rights, most teachers avoided or diverted students' comments or simply stated "that's the way things were." Rather than create or use opportunities to engage and/or challenge students' thinking about inequality, most teachers silenced students' inquiry and curiosity, leaving questions unanswered and students frustrated. By avoiding discussions and activities about the significance of racism and limitations on rights throughout history, the teachers missed several opportunities to challenge and broaden students' thinking.

Pedagogical Constraints on Teaching National History for Social Justice

Standards and Testing

In Oakdale and elsewhere, teaching U.S. history for social justice faces many challenges and constraints. State learning standards and curricular frameworks present nationalist interpretations of U.S. history and pressure teachers into teaching to the test (Conrbleth & Waugh, 1995; Grant, 2003, 2006; Loewen, 1995; Nash, Crabtree & Dunn, 2000; Sleeter, 2005; Sleeter & Stillman, 2005; Symcox, 2002). Among others, California, Michigan and New York state social studies learning standards and curricular frameworks present nationalist interpretations of U.S. history yet expect students to become citizens who respect and participate in democratic practices. Yet the frameworks make little mention of the myriad ways that the nation perpetrated racism and other forms of inequality or of the ways that students today can challenge inequality beyond the traditional means of voting, volunteering and/or joining political parties. Textbooks reinforce dominant views of national development in which racism receded, rights expanded and the United States is the most enlightened nation in the world today.

State testing in history, social studies and other subjects based on state learning standards also pressure teachers to teach state-sanctioned interpretations on national history. Testing has led history and social studies teachers to create or revise curricula which correlate closely with state tests and has led history and social studies teachers to narrow the curricular topics covered in class (Grant, 2006; Segall, 2006; Van Hover, 2006). Testing has affected the curricular practices of new teachers particularly. One study found that new teachers responded to the overwhelming list of concepts and ideas embedded in standards by moving superficially from topic to topic, rather than by determining which ideas were worthy of in-depth study (Kaufman, Johnson, Kardos, Liu, & Peske, 2002). Experienced history teachers also have been pressured to teach to the tests and like new teachers, have responded by adapting classroom lessons and units to the content and themes reflected in state standards (Segall, 2006).

White Teachers' and Students' Avoidance of "Race Talk"

As noted in Chapter 1, white teachers and students often avoid "race talk" in racially homogenous and diverse classrooms. Some teachers believe that race is too controversial to discuss, especially with younger children or in mixed race classrooms; others fear offending students and/or their parents, engendering racial divisiveness among students or alienating students from affiliating positively with a national identity. Many pre-service or experienced teachers lack and/or reject information about institutional racism and/or see contemporary racism as individual rather than institutional in nature. As a consequence of their knowledge and beliefs, many teachers continue to teach about racial groups' contributions and experiences intermittently or present racism and other forms of violence and exclusion as exceptions rather than integral to the nation's progressive development.

As a result of teachers' and the larger mainstream community's avoidance of discussions of race, white students also have had difficulty talking about race or acknowledging racism as institutional in nature. Many believe that although individual prejudice exits, institutional racism does not, or worse, whites are now the victims of "reverse racism." Others take refuge in concepts of meritocracy and share a "blame the victim" mentality. Out of guilt, fear, hatred and/or ignorance white children, adolescents and adults in single or mixed raced classroom settings have found it difficult to discuss racism and many simply fall silent when issues about racism are raised.

Given these constraints, how might history teachers and educators make headway in assisting practicing and pre-service teachers to bridge racial and other divides in children's and adolescents' historical interpretations? How might teachers become more aware of the relationship between their own and their students' sociocultural identities and interpretive frameworks, gain greater access to curricular approaches and materials which present more critical accounts of U.S. history and contemporary society, and create opportunities in class to educate, challenge and ultimately broaden students' knowledge and beliefs? And how might teachers relate historical issues to contemporary problems so that students see both continuity and change in racism and rights over time and give students a sense of agency to challenge or change the status quo? In short, how might teachers teach history for social justice?

Possibilities for Pedagogical Change

Teachers' Awareness of their Interpretive Frameworks

To enable teachers to become aware of how their racial identities have shaped their interpretations of U.S. history and society, they can complete a condensed version of the nation narration task—selecting and explaining important historical actors and events—used in this study. When working with pre-service teachers, I've asked them to list, explain, and discuss the most important people and events in U.S. history from a list of 20 actors/events. We've discussed their selections and explanations and examined race-ethnic related differences in responses. In instances where all or the vast majority of pre-service teachers have been white, I've asked them to complete the exercise and then read my article (Epstein, 2000) on the differences in white and black adolescents' interpretations of history. The exercise enabled white pre-service teachers to become aware of more than their own interpretive frameworks. They've also become more cognizant of the racialized or ideological nature of historical interpretations. Even white pre-service teachers who recognized the extent of racism towards people of color historically and considered racism to be a major problem today remarked on the difference between their more abstract and less bounded articulations of racism and the more visceral and overarching responses to racial violence that the black adolescents in the 2000 study had articulated. In classes where I've taught African American, Latino and white pre-service teachers, the white students acknowledged that race-related differences in historical and contemporary interpretations are just as prevalent today and among well educated adults as they were in Oakdale. Black and Latino students, on the other hand, had become more assertive and authoritative class participants as their knowledge about the effects of racial identity on interpretation and the marginalization of their knowledge and beliefs have been affirmed.

Teachers' Awareness of Students' Interpretive Frames

Teachers who understand the interpretive frames that children or adolescents bring to historical inquiry may be better able to teach to and beyond their knowledge and beliefs. By asking students to complete modified versions of the nation narration task at the beginning of the year, teachers can gain immediate information on students' existing content and concept knowledge, misconceptions and beliefs. They can then plan pedagogical strategies to reaffirm, challenge and/or extend students' understandings. In classrooms where students see racism as intermittent, for example, teachers can ask questions and present lessons about how racism operated in every era of U.S. history, as well as today, and include examples of how people as individuals and groups resisted inequality. Similarly, teachers can present the extension of rights over time as something that expanded *and* contracted and as something which people continue to struggle for today.

Teachers also can ask students to complete the modified versions of the nation narration task at the end of a unit or year to assess if or how instruction shaped or changed students' explanations and interpretations and to plan instruction in subsequent years. Another way to acquire the information is to ask students at the beginning and end of a curricular unit to complete the KWL activity (what students *know* about a historical actor and event, what they *want* to know, what they *learn*). Tasks like KWL and the nation narration task provide immediate and long-term feedback on how teachers' pedagogical practices challenged, reinforced and/or extended students' historical and political understandings.

Research studies have demonstrated that black, Mexican American and Native American adolescents and adults have constructed more critical interpretations of U.S. history, contemporary society and history taught in schools than have whites (Almarza, 2001; Barton & Levstik, 1998; Bonilla-Silva, 2003; Epstein, 1998, 2000; Rosenzweig & Thelen, 1998; Rubin, 2007; Kinder & Sanders, 1997; Sears, Sianius & Bobo, 2000; Schuman, Steeh, Bobo & Krysan, 1997). Teachers and teacher educators can use the research as a reference point for creating history lessons which acknowledge students' interpretive frameworks and reinforce or challenge their interpretations of race and rights. For example, to affirm the interpretive frameworks of students of color, teachers can integrate themes throughout each unit of study of the ongoing and institutional nature of racism. In the case of African Americans, teachers can include lessons on the existence of slavery in northern colonies, something that many Americans are not aware of. Similarly, lynching of black men and other forms of intimidation occurred in the North and South, as did race riots in the North, Midwest and West during the nineteenth and twentieth centuries. Local, state, and national governments—as well as individuals—used a vast array of legal and extra-legal means to have kept or keep black people and other people of color oppressed. Teachers can use the problems with black access to voting in Florida during the 2000 election to remind students that individuals and governments still use dirty tricks to deny fundamental rights to people of color. Overall, teachers need to move beyond typical lessons on the African slave trade, slavery, segregation and the Civil Rights Movement to supplement all students' sketchy and victim-oriented knowledge of black historical experiences, as well as challenge white students' understanding of racism as intermittent, relatively devoid of violence and individually perpetrated or non-existent today.

Teachers also need to work with and against state learning standards in teaching about the contributions that people of different races and ethnicities have made to national history. Black history is not just the history of an enslaved, segregated and violated people; it is the story of a people's struggle for freedom and equality which has benefited all Americans not originally designated as voting members of a democracy (Franklin & Moss, 2000; Horton & Horton, 2001). Black slave and free labor contributed enormously to the development of industry, transportation, science and technology, as well as to the American Revolution and Civil War. Black writers and artists have flourished before, during and after the Harlem Renaissance and their poetry, paintings and stories can be integrated into the curriculum to tell in vivid terms stories of racism and racism resisted, as well as to connect to broader themes about American life. The contributions of Asian Americans, Mexican Americans and Native Americans to the economy, politics, and cultural life are an integral and neglected part of the story of national development; internet access to historical and contemporary writings, visuals, documents and audio sources by or about people of color are available to teachers and students even in underfunded schools (see section on Resources).

Teachers also can elaborate upon themes already familiar to students. While most acknowledge that African Americans acquired greater rights for blacks and other Americans during the Civil Rights Movement, black political action occurred as early as the eighteenth century. Enslaved and free blacks in the North and South authored petitions to state governments for freedom, greater equality and even repatriation to Africa. Slave labor not just built much of the Southern infrastructure of waterways, roads, railroads and agriculture; slave labor also was responsible for contributing to agricultural and manufacturing development in the North and to providing profits which were used to fund European soldiers who fought and helped to win the American Revolution. Black men fought on both sides of the conflict in the American Revolution and the American Revolution freed more slaves than any other event before the Civil War (Franklin & Moss, 2000, Horton & Horton, 2001). Black men and women fought for freedom and rights before and after the Civil War and contributed to the expansion of national concepts of freedom and equality (Foner, 1999). Blacks as a people contributed to the nation's political, economic, social and cultural development of the nation throughout the nineteenth and twentieth centuries. Including these forgotten chapters may create greater trust among black students in school-based historical narratives and greater respect among white students for black contributions.

Dominant historical narratives also tell too few tales about white actors who fought for freedom or equality for blacks and other people of color or who joined interracial movements. Biographies of white allies (Brown, 2002) contain lessons about individual courage and conviction and historical examples of cross-racial movements for black freedom exist beyond abolitionism and the Civil Rights Movement. Black and white farmers created separate but parallel and cooperative alliances during the late nineteenth century and interracial alliances during the 1930s. White and black men both participated in the Populist Party in the nineteenth century and the Communist Party in the twentieth century, and a few unions such as the United Mine Workers organized black and white workers. Although these and other organizations reflected racist tensions and practices, they provide examples for black students that white actors and groups at times crossed racial lines to support blacks. White allies and organizations also provide white students with role models of individuals and groups which stood up against racism and other forms of inequality, even when it was unpopular or dangerous.

Teachers in mixed race classrooms also can use racial differences in students' interpretive frameworks to illustrate the ideological nature of history and all school knowledge. In another study in Ms. Hines' class (Epstein, 2000), I presented eleventh graders with data on race-related differences in students' beliefs about the credibility of secondary historical sources. I asked students to explain why white students believed that history textbooks, teachers, and library books were the most credible sources of history, and why black students believed that family members, black teachers, and movies or documentaries by or about blacks ranked highest. White students speculated that black students were closer to their families and spent more time with and learning from family members. Black students thought it was because teachers and textbooks did not tell "the whole story" about national history and they had to learn about black experiences and contributions from family and black-oriented sources. Some white students rethought their original assumptions about the causes of black students' credibility rankings, prompting one to acknowledge that "I guess we really didn't learn that much about black people this year."

Using student responses to the nation narration or KWL task, teachers can present similar data to students in their own classes. Differences in students' knowledge, questions, and beliefs about historical actors or events can serve as an opening for discussions about the relationship between power and school knowledge generally, and the relationship among school-based interpretations of history and white power and privilege specifically (Anderson, 1994; Holt, 1995; Segall, 1999). Having students analyze the results of these tasks also may engender respect for students of different races/ethnicities as students from dominant groups begin to learn what students from marginalized groups know about history and what they want to learn.

Creating Pedagogy based on Knowledge of Students' Interpretive Frames

Knowledge of students' interpretive frames can assist teachers in producing culturally responsive pedagogy (Ladson-Billings, 1995) aimed at broadening the historical interpretations of students of color and white students. As a secondary social studies methods professor and leader of professional development workshops, I've asked pre-service and practicing teachers to read and discuss my 2000 article on racial differences in adolescents' historical interpretations. They then created lesson plans which supported and extended students' historical understandings about race relations and connected past issues about race to contemporary issues. Teachers created lesson plans which had students learn about and debate racism in the military, politics, schooling and the media in the past and today. One teacher created a plan asking students to debate whether the national government should provide African Americans with reparations for enslavement. She included readings on the government's compensation of Asian Americans for property loss during World War II as historical context and comparison, as well as articles by contemporary African American writers who argued for and against reparations (Epstein, 2002). Others had students debate complementary and competing strategies that African Americans have developed for combating racism, and included examples from the works of Booker T. Washington, W. E. B. Dubois, Fannie Lou Hamer, Martin Luther King, Jr., and Malcolm X. The teachers I've worked with have responded well to these assignments, recognizing that many students of color in urban schools become energized by discussions around race and resistance and that all students learn about the various strategies which leaders have invoked to gain greater freedom and rights.

Teachers also can present racial group experiences from multiple perspectives, including those of "indigenous insiders" (Banks, 2004b) or writers who've written about the experiences or subject matter from the perspectives of the communities from which their students originate. Sleeter (2005) had pre-service teachers read historical accounts that discussed oppression, racial conflict, and racial groups' subjectivity in the face of oppression. She presented examples of pre-service teachers who moved beyond the "cultural differences" approach of teaching about Native American tribes to having created units in which elementary students investigated conflicts between Native Americans and European Americans related to land use and hunting. Many state curricular standards prescribe teaching the history of Native American tribes in elementary schools, and turning teachers' attention to Native Americans' perspectives on white-Native American historical relationships or Native American perspectives on contemporary problems in their communities can broaden their own and their students' knowledge base.

Older students might benefit also from critical accounts of historical texts or textbooks about well known figures and events. By showing students the limitations of textbook narrative accounts—how they oversimplify, omit and marginalize controversial topics or events—students learn that history is more complex and national history more problematic than most high school history textbooks portray. Derrick Alridge (2006), for example, analyzed the portrayal of Martin Luther King, Jr. in popular high school history textbooks, and illustrated how the texts ignore the multidimensional and radical aspects of King's beliefs. Similarly, Diana Hess (2005) critiqued textbook accounts of *Brown vs. Board of Education* Supreme Court decision, which have stripped the decision of historical and contemporary controversy. By reading articles which critique textbook accounts or by engaging in other exercises which illustrate the limits of textbook narratives, adolescents might become more critical consumers of all historical texts, as well as more knowledgeable about the state's purpose in presenting positive portrayals of the nation, at the expense of more accurate and full bodied accounts (Segall, 2006).

Curricular Materials and Approaches

Although history teachers have an obligation to ensure that students learn the historical information required to pass state exams, they also have an obligation to teach about national history in ways that reflect the experiences, interpretations, and interactions of the nation's diverse population. Professional opportunities which present alternative interpretations of U.S. history provide great avenues for professional development. Although the federal government's *Teaching American History Grant* program specifies that the grant's purpose is to "promote the teaching of traditional American history" so that "students will

develop an appreciation for the great ideas of American history"
(www.ed.gov/programs/teachinghistory), some grant recipients
provide readings, speakers and visits to historical sites and museums
which present multiple and/or critical interpretations. Local, regional,
state and national museums and historic sites also present alternative
interpretations of controversial historical topics and many, at the very
least, present the contributions and experiences of people of color and
other non-elites. Museums and cultural centers by or about African
Americans and other people of color exist in every region of the country
and most have educational programs and guides for assisting teachers
in pre- and post-museum visits with students. Some, like the New York
Historical Society (www.slaveryinnewyork.org), have developed online
professional development programs where teachers and students can
interact with the website to learn about the history of slavery in New
York and other northern cities.

Professional organizations also disseminate materials for teachers to
supplement state-sanctioned history-social studies curricula and provide
more complex or controversial interpretations of the nation's history. The
American Historical Association's *The History Teacher*, National Council
for the Social Studies' *Social Education* and *Social Studies for the Young
Learner*, the Organization of American Historians' *Magazine of History*,
Rethinking Schools (www.rethinkingschools.org), Facing History and
Ourselves (www.facinghistory.org) and Teaching for Change (www.
teachingforchange.org) websites and publications offer information,
strategies and materials for presenting critical and professionally sound
historical interpretations on topics related to diversity and democracy.
Websites which include primary documents or documentaries related
to black historical experiences have exploded and include the Library
of Congress' *Resource Guide for the Study of Black History and Culture*
(www.loc.gov/exhibits/african/intro.html); New York Public Library's
Schomborg Center for Research on Black Culture (www.nypl.org/research/sc/
sc.html); Gilder-Lehrman Center for the Study of Slavery, Resistance and
Abolition at Yale University (www.gilderlehrman.org/institute/slavery.
html); PBS's *Africans in America* documentary series (www.pbs.org/wgbh/
aia); Cornell University's *Guide to African American Documentary Resources*
(www.people.cornell.edu/pages/elw25/aa_digital_archiveshome.htm)
and the University of Washington Libraries African American History

page (www.lib.washington.edu/subject/History/tm/black.html). Similar organizations and websites exist for other racial-ethnic groups and can supplement textbooks and state learning standards.

Community-based organizations, neighborhood- or community-oriented museums, and community members and events which highlight the history and ongoing experiences of marginalized groups are another means for teachers to learn about racial-ethnic group interpretations and experiences; mainstream museums, historical sites, and other locations also offer special or permanent exhibits related to the histories of marginalized groups, race relations and/or limits and extensions of rights. Many museums have books, videos, speaker series and other activities which present history and contemporary issues from multiple perspectives and which critique mainstream or dominant presentations of the past and present.

Creating Classroom Cultures for Discussions of Race

Setting Ground Rules for Discussion

Classroom discussions around racially and politically charged issues are difficult and those which relate to differences in students' racial-ethnic identities can be especially difficult to conduct. Teachers in multiracial classrooms often invoke their authority to promote the absence of discussions related to race, redirect racially or politically charged discussions towards safe or safer topics or abstract concepts, or maintain a relativist stance in which all comments, except the most egregious, are tacitly accepted (Bolgatz, 2003; Dickar, in press; Fine, 1993; Lewis, 2003; McIntyre, 1997). Despite the difficulties, discussions about race relations, especially in U.S. history classes, are necessary both in racially homogenous and racially diverse classrooms. Studies of social studies classes (Avery & Hahn, 2004) have demonstrated that teachers who maintained "open classroom climates," i.e. provided opportunities in class for students to voice their views on controversial topics, maintained guidelines about respectful speech and turn taking, and held their own views on the topics in check had greater success at creating tolerance among students for a diversity of views. At the same time, teachers also have to guide and challenge students in their discussions about race so that racist attitudes and views are disrupted (Fine, 1993).

In discussing issues related to race and other sensitive issues, teachers in high school (Bolgatz, 2005; Fine, 1995) and college (Sleeter, 2005) classrooms have implemented a set of ground rules. These include building trust with students and between students before introducing controversial issues; accepting without necessarily agreeing with others' interpretations or points of view; speaking from one's own experience and accepting others' interpretations of their experiences as valid; allowing speakers to complete their comments without interruption; seeking clarification of students' views and asking them to provide evidence; expressing disagreement between students respectfully; and having students make distinctions between disagreements with others' points of views and negative judgments about the speaker or his/her point of view. Flinders University in Australia has a comprehensive website on strategies for teaching about controversial issues (www. flinders.edu.au/teach/t4l/inclusive/controversial.php), as does the Street Law Organization in Silver Spring, Maryland (www.streetlaw. org/controversy2.html).

Teachers who use a set of ground rules or guidelines with students to set the parameters of discussions around controversial issues may not always succeed. Fine (1993, 1995) conducted a case study of a high school teacher who had her students subscribe to these guidelines in discussions of Middle Eastern history and contemporary Arab-Israeli conflicts. While the teacher managed the discussion well by asking students to clarify meanings and distinguish between personal opinion and fact, the teacher also fell short of the ideal facilitator. Fine credited the teacher with having constructed a classroom environment in which she encouraged students to represent their views on controversial issues and where students felt safe enough to express unpopular views which might (and did) offend Jewish American students in the class (who themselves represented diverse views). But she also exposed the teacher's limitations—which she represented as an inevitably human response—in favoring the students whose views were similar to hers by having given them more time to speak, allowed them to go unchallenged, become the last comment of the day, etc. The point is that although it is impossible for teachers always to enact a fair balance in classroom discussions, teachers who think of the discussions as learning experiences for themselves, as well as for their students, can still provide opportunities for moving towards understanding racial divides.

Begin with Less Controversial Topics

In classrooms where students are not accustomed to talking about difference or dealing with conflict, it may be easier to engage students in discussions about racism or religious oppression which do not involve the identities of students in the class and in which they might not feel personally involved or open to attack. White students in Oakdale, for example, acknowledged white racism towards Native Americans more readily than white racism towards blacks, with the exception of slavery. The fact that there were no Native American students in the classroom, as well as few or no Native American students in the school district might have made it easier for white and black students to discuss Native American oppression. In addition, white and black students had no personal experiences with Native Americans. Many of the white and fewer black students also saw racism towards Native Americans as a past or distant problem which didn't relate to them personally. History teachers might use acknowledgment of racism towards Native Americans—a theme as old and enduring as the beginning of interracial contact in the Americas in the fifteenth century—as a springboard for subsequent discussions of whites' roles in the racial exploitation of others.

It's also important when working with white students that teachers make a distinction between holding whites in contemporary society responsible for past racism and holding whites accountable for past oppression. Grant (2003), for example, found that white high school students were less resistant to discussing white racism historically when the black teacher made clear that they and other whites in contemporary society were not being blamed or directly held responsible for past acts of racism. At the same time, teachers need to educate white students on the way in which *whites as a group* are accountable in big (i.e. racial disparities in income, health, housing, occupations, prison sentencing, etc.) and small (followed by security in stores and malls, stopped by police on streets and highways, asked for identification when using credit cards, etc. See McIntosh, 1990) for the privileges they are accorded as a result of their status as the dominant racial group.

Writing and Reflecting before Speaking

Teachers can provide class time or assign homework which enables students to think through and justify their positions on race-related issues and/or respond to the positions of other classmates or materials with whom or which they disagree. Fine (1995) and Bolgatz (2005) found that students explored their ideas about race more fully and honestly when they had time to reflect and revise their thinking and could examine unpopular views without publicly exposing their ideas and beliefs. Although the writing practices did not result in immediate changes in students' views, it assisted students in clarifying their views and enabled them to raise and reflect on ideas in safe spaces. Teachers also can use students' writing as guides to introducing topics and gently challenging students' beliefs. To challenge students who believe that racism doesn't exist or that it is individual in nature, for example, a teacher can bring in statistics which show the disparities between whites and people of color in income, health care, high school retention and graduation, and prison sentencing. and have students discuss possible explanations for the disparities. By having students write about their knowledge and beliefs about race, teachers can challenge students' racist beliefs without publicly responding to individual students as having made racist statements.

Begin with Discussion of Race and Identity

In classrooms where students are comfortable talking about race, teachers can begin the year with discussions and activities about race, identity, history and contemporary society. Currently, I am conducting a study with two New York City teachers cited for their effectiveness in integrating discussions of race and race relations into their history classes with black and Latino student populations (Epstein, 2007a). Working with students who are aware of and affected on a daily basis by racism, both teachers began the school year with a two-week unit on race and identity. The teachers' purposes were many—they wanted to create a trusting yet frank environment for discussions about race; they knew that their students were not only interested in the topic but possessed both anecdotal knowledge and analytic skills to interpret and discuss race relations; and they believed that students' insights into their identities as people from marginalized racial groups were necessary for students' survival and success. Most significantly, however, both teachers underscored the idea that young people can't be considered educated without an understanding of the racial dynamics of national development and contemporary society. Talking or teaching about U.S. history and society without teaching about race is "nonsensical," in the words of one teacher and "impossible," in the view of the other.

Each teacher began the class in September by asking students to define race, identify themselves racially, ethnically and nationally, and describe how they "know" when someone is of or from a particular racial group or groups. They also asked the students to define and describe an "American." Most of the students explained race as a biological construct, considered themselves to be African American, Puerto Rican, Dominican, Dominican and African American, etc., but did not identify themselves as Americans. They used surface bodily features as indicators of a person's race/ethnicity, and defined American as those who are "blonde haired, blued eyed and speak without an accent." The teachers then introduced through readings and videos concepts of race as socially constructed and changes in racial categorization over time. One teacher had students watch a documentary tracing people's DNA which illustrated the mixed raced ancestry of famous African Americans. The other had students read parts of Cornell West's *Race Matters* which delineated the differences between and significance of the social and material conditions of racial categories. The teachers also had students examine "race" beyond those who are designated as black and white, and several Asian American students in one class described the stereotypes and epithets that blacks, Latinos and white children and adolescents have hurled at them.

In addition, the teachers have included the experiences of racial groups in every unit. The teachers included black experiences and perspectives on the American Revolution by having students read sources on blacks who fought with and against the colonists. They included complex discussions about black-white relations during slavery, invoking sophisticated conversations about whether black women who became white masters' mistresses ever loved or cared for their enslavers or the range of black men's choices and emotions and the consequences of their choices in responding to white violence. They incorporated discussions of contemporary racist incidents like the Jena 6 case, and encouraged rather than silenced student initiated discussions of local incidents—the shooting of black men by the police, a common occurrence in many parts of the United States. After students expressed their opinions and often their anger, the teachers asked them what they might do to lessen racial violence and police mistreatment and/or protect themselves and their communities from racist attacks. In short, these exemplary teachers accepted, challenged and integrated students' knowledge and experiences of racism into the history curriculum, providing space to discuss and learn about the complexities of and responses to racial experiences.

Dealing with Emotional Aspects of Race and Racism

White students and students of color often have different emotional responses to discussions about race. In Oakdale and elsewhere, white students felt guilty and defensive about racism and preferred to avoid or fell silent during discussions of race. In mixed race classrooms, they often felt blamed by students of color for the nation's racist legacy and responded defensively by noting, more often in private than public, that they or their ancestors aren't to blame for what happened in the past. In majority white classrooms, white students' political discourses about race are connected to emotional defensiveness, which often leads them to deny, underestimate or blame "other" white people for racism (Trainor, 2005). Black students in Oakdale exhibited anger when their teachers discussed (and avoided discussions) of slavery and segregation; others have suggested (Payne, 2003) that black students have been ashamed to talk about slavery particularly and other examples of black subordination historically. I've also heard Chinese American students in New York City schools express anger about the amount of time that teachers spend on black history and frustration at the lack of lessons about the Chinese experience in national history

Teachers who recognize students' and their own emotional responses to racism in U.S. history may be better able to release or at least bring to the surface troubled and troubling feelings. One way to do this is to ask students to discuss their feelings towards historical actors and events. One of the effective teachers I currently observe began the unit on slavery with a complex picture of the slave trade (http://africanhistory.about.com/od/slaveryimages/ig/Slavery-Images-Gallery) and asked students to distinguish among what they *see* in the picture (i.e. a description of the visual), what they *think* is going on in the picture (analysis) and what they *feel* in response to the picture (emotional response). After students discussed their responses, the teacher acknowledged that students would feel a range of emotions—and particularly anger—as they studied slavery. As a Puerto Rican and American, she said she too felt angry at the dehumanization of Africans and African Americans and still found it difficult to delve into slavery's past. In recognizing students' and her own feelings about racism, however, she enabled students to publicly display their feelings, acknowledging that racism past or present still creates pain. Teachers in majority white classrooms similarly can acknowledge and provide space for feelings of denial and guilt, recognizing the difficulty that white people have in dealing with racism.

Examples of Effective Teachers

Effective History Teacher of Middle Class White Students

Teachers who remind white students that they personally are not to blame for the history of white racism, connect the history of white-black relations to other examples of oppression, and provide examples of historical and contemporary agency to challenge racism may find some success in making white students less resistant to studying the history of race relations in the United States and more open to reflecting on their own role as potential change agents. Grant (2003) reported on a history teacher in an upscale white suburban community in upstate New York who designed a month long unit on the Civil Rights Movement. In planning the unit, the teacher had several purposes in mind. She wanted to show students how racism operated in daily life; that people in the past and present held multiple perspectives; the power of individuals and groups to change society; and how racism was one of many forms of discrimination that operated in the past and present. She used a range of pedagogical techniques and related the Civil Rights Movement to discrimination against homosexuals in today's society.

As an African American woman, Ms. Strait also was aware of white students' sensitivities about "blaming whites" for racism and made a distinction between people in the past who were responsible for racism and people in contemporary society who are not responsible for past racism and had agency in not perpetuating oppression in contemporary society. The students in Ms. Strait's class responded positively to her lessons, in part because she did not hold all whites responsible for racism and related racism to other forms of oppression. Consequently, students felt less defensive about their white identities, as well as about the singular impact of racism as a marker of inequality and they were able to compare different forms of discrimination historically and today. While some students responded with naïve optimism about how much the nation had changed since the 1950s and 1960s, others recognized that racism, homophobia and other forms of oppression still existed and changes in laws or policies alone had not resulted in equality.

Ms. Strait's stance that whites in contemporary society should not be held responsible for racism in the past, as well as her emphasis on students' agency to challenge racism today, prompted some students to examine their racial privilege. A few expressed discomfort or uncertainty about knowing how to act or behave in settings that were not majority white, saw their experiences in an all white suburb as somewhat limiting, and questioned whether they would resist or stand up against discriminatory remarks or practices if they arose. In past years, when Ms. Strait incorporated black experiences into her lessons, white students became very resistant and believed that she was blaming whites for racism. Ms. Strait found that by connecting racism against blacks historically with other historic and contemporary forms of oppression, white students were more open to accepting the historical and contemporary effects of white privilege, racism against people of color, and other forms of oppression.

Effective Humanities Teacher of Poor Students of Color

Chris Gutierrez (2000), a teacher in South Central Los Angeles, wanted to enable eleventh graders to connect national history to their lives in ways that enabled them to feel empowered to act upon community problems individually and collectively. She came to these goals during a time when she recognized that African American, Latino and Cambodian American students in her classes continually blamed whites for past and contemporary problems and saw themselves and their communities as victims of oppression. She wondered if or how the overarching curricular theme of her U.S. history and literature class—"Image versus Reality of the American Experiment"—which focused on the gap between national ideals of democracy and the realities of oppression, gave too little emphasis to historical agency and how people in oppressive contexts acted to resist oppression. She changed the course theme to "Individual Rights and Responsibilities in a Multicultural Democracy" and focused students' attention on the relationship between the broad economic, political, and social forces which structured historical events and periods, as well as the role of individual and group agency in changing historical circumstances.

To bring these concepts to life at the beginning of the year, she placed two drawings on the board. One was a stick figure in a three dimensional box with closed sides. The box represented the range of historical or contemporary forces which shaped individual or group circumstances during particular events or periods, i.e. that people's life circumstances and opportunities are shaped by the larger society. The second box was of an individual inside a three dimensional box in which s/he partially pushed open one side of the box. The purpose of the second box was to have students think about the means at people's disposal to change their circumstances. She used the visual heuristics as a means to have students analyze what historical and contemporary actors (including themselves) and groups have done to transform oppressive conditions, even if they are not capable of changing the entirety of factors related to race or class.

In addition, Ms. Gutierrez asked students to consider not just the actions and motivations of historical actors, but how they would have acted had they been present during the event or period. Not only did the exercise make history less of an abstract narrative about "dead people," but a more humanistic inquiry about people's motivations and agency. It also prompted students to become more reflective about the decisions they made in their own lives and about the kinds of actions they could imagine or implement as community members oriented towards change. The themes and questions that the teacher posed prompted one student to write in a response to a question about how the study of the past related to students' lives, "I also realize that when I succeed, I can come back to my own community and give it a hand so that young kids will wake up to see a better future" (p. 373).

Lessons of Research on Effective Teachers

Teachers who connect the nation's history of oppression and unequal rights to the struggles of women, immigrants, gay people, and other disenfranchised groups may enable white students to move beyond the guilt or defensiveness associated with white privilege and students of color to move beyond anger or feelings of victimization by recognizing that before the twentieth century, greater numbers of Americans experienced oppression or disenfranchisement than were granted rights or equality (Keyssar, 2000; Smith, 1997). They also illustrate the benefits of relating past oppression to contemporary forms of exclusion, asking students to reflect on their decision-making processes in the same or analogous circumstances, and instilling in students a sense of agency by presenting individual and group strategies for standing up against racism and other forms of oppression (see Facing History and Ourselves and Rethinking Schools websites and publications for curriculum materials and pedagogical approaches).

Schools and school districts can do more to enable individual teachers to learn about race in history and society as part of a larger community. Some schools have established school improvement committees and teacher study groups devoted to working with and through issues related to racism, sexism, homophobia, etc. and ongoing contact and sponsorship of events with groups like the NAACP, Anti-Defamation League, National Organization for Women, etc. represent district-wide support. While revisions of teachers' pedagogical practices are a necessary means to interrupt racist portrayals of history and society, teachers and schools which examine and reform structures throughout the school and the district to break down forms of hierarchy and inequality reinforce classroom efforts at examining and challenging inequality (Lewis, 2003; Pollock, 2004).

Conclusion

Teaching about race-related differences in the interpretations of U.S. history, as well as examining the role of racism and the struggle by diverse people in every historical period to extend equal rights presents a more honest and accurate account of our national legacy. It also contributes to a major purpose of teaching U.S. history for social justice. More honest discussions about racial oppression and struggle may lead students to construct more realistic views of national history and identity. Teaching history in ways that promote the examination of the failings of the nation's past, as well as its virtues, may better equip young people to acknowledge and understand the roots of contemporary racism and inequality, to learn about the existence and effectiveness of cross-racial alliances, and to imagine themselves and act as citizens capable of change in contemporary society. Using, rather than avoiding, race-related differences in young people's interpretive frames provides ground rules and structures for discussions of controversial issues and gives students practice in the kinds of deliberative democracy that Americans must undergo in a diverse and unequal state (Parker, 2006).

If we care to involve all of the nation's students in the study of their pasts, current concepts of history education must move beyond the acquisition of state-sanctioned interpretations or disciplinary dispositions and methods towards more critical and participatory democratic goals. The attempt to create patriotic citizens through the presentation of sanitized versions of the nation's past at best works against teaching young people to assess and synthesize critically historical texts and at worst further alienates young people who don't believe the state's interpretations, no matter how often dominant perspectives are presented. Conversely, expecting students to become "little historians" without reference to whose or which history they are learning does not acknowledge the shortcomings of state-sanctioned interpretations of race and rights historically or today, and leaves unchallenged whose or which historical questions and texts are promoted by schools and society. If national history in the twenty-first century is to have a positive and educative effect on all of the nation's young, history teachers, policy makers and researchers need to address more directly and deeply the relationships among young people's social identities, the roles of racism and inequality in national history and life, and contemporary aims of citizenship education in a multicultural society. Only by forging and re-forging these connections can history education live up to its potential as a basis for constructing concepts of national identities and citizenship to which all students can relate and aspire.

Appendix A: Fifth Grade Picture Cards

Native American Tribes–1500

European Exploration

Christopher Columbus

Slavery

American Revolution

George Washington

Founding Fathers

Constitution

Bill of Rights

Harriet Tubman

Underground Railroad

Civil War

Abraham Lincoln

Rosa Parks

Martin Luther King, Jr.

Malcolm X

Appendix B: Picture Cards for Eighth and Eleventh Graders

1500s–1865

Native American Tribes

European Exploration

Christopher Columbus

Slave Trade

Crispus Attucks

American Revolution

Declaration of Independence

Constitution

Bill of Rights

Founding Fathers

George Washington

Growth of United States

Growth of Slavery

Slave Rebellions

Harriet Tubman

Underground Railroad

Civil War

Blacks in Civil War

Abraham Lincoln

Emancipation Proclamation

1865–1970s

Westward Movement

Native American Reservations

Segregation in the South

European Immigration

Black Migration

Invention of Automobile

Invention of Airplane

Women's Suffrage

The Great Depression

World War II

Blacks in World War II

Women in World War II

Japanese Internment Camps

Atom Bomb

Rosa Parks

Martin Luther King, Jr.

Malcolm X

Civil Rights Movement

John F. Kennedy

Vietnam War

Protest Against Vietnam War

Nixon's Resignation

Appendix C: Research Methods

Initial Questionnaire

The research task and methods first used with eleventh grade students in two of Ms. Hines' classes in June1994, developed over the years. I was interested in learning what white and black students thought was significant in U.S. history. I began with a questionnaire, asking 46 students in the two classes to select and explain three important actors and events in U.S. history (Epstein, 1998). I coded students' explanations deductively and inductively, categorizing explanations of George Washington as the "first president" or the Civil War as "having unified the country" under the code of "nation building"; those of Martin Luther King, Jr., as "had a dream for African Americans" or "gave African Americans rights" under "African American experiences"; the Declaration of Independence or Constitution as "having given people rights" as "individual rights," etc.

From the analysis, I found that two-thirds of the white students' responses related to nation building and rights combined and 22 percent related to African American experiences. Conversely, two-thirds of the black students' explanations related to African American experiences and 25 percent related to nation building and rights combined. In some instances, even when white and black students selected the same historical actor or event, they had different explanations. For example, both groups selected John F. Kennedy as significant, but white students more often explained his importance in terms of his assistance to "ordinary people" or the "revival of patriotism," while black students cited the fact that he "helped black people" or "helped black people and that's why they shot him." Similarly, white and black students selected King and the Civil Rights Movement as important. White students, however, described King and the Civil Rights Movement as having "got rights for blacks", while black students described them as having "got rights for blacks" *and* as having "ended the fighting between blacks and whites."

Nation Narration Task

While I found these differences to be significant and intriguing, I wanted to learn more. How did students explain or interpret the "whole" of U.S. history and what might that tell us about how young people's lived experiences and family histories, as well as the teacher's instruction, influenced their views of the past? William Purves, a doctoral student at the University of Michigan at the time, and I designed a research task to elicit students' "interpretive frames." Students would be given an assortment of "picture cards" of historical actors and events which spanned the course of U.S. history and asked to select and explain the most important. I also asked them to review their selections and explanations and discuss what had and had not changed over the course of national development.

In selecting actors/events for the task, I included traditional nation building or altering actors and events, such as presidents, founding documents, wars, and those related to technological advances. I also included actors/events related to African American experiences throughout the course of national history. This enabled students to create a national history that included multiple combinations of historical actors and events to create a narrative that ranged from depicting an entirely or primarily traditional nation building narrative, a narrative focused solely or primarily on African American experiences, or any combination thereof. All of the actors/events included would be those that the teacher had discussed in class.

The following May (1995), I returned to Ms. Hines' classroom. Black doctoral students interviewed 10 black students and I interviewed 10 white students (who varied in academic achievement) and asked them to imagine they were creating a textbook for young people like themselves. The task was divided into three parts: first students selected and explained from a set of 24 pictures the 10 most important actors and events in U.S. history, beginning with Native American settlement and continuing through Reconstruction. Next, they selected and explained

10 of 28 important actors/events from the late nineteenth century through Nixon's resignation. They then reviewed their selections and discussed what had and had not changed over the centuries.

Data Analysis

To analyze explanations of individual actors/events, I created deductive and inductive codes, expanding upon the ones used with the questionnaires. In coding explanations about the Bill of Rights, for example, students' explanations fell into two or three categories: those that defined rights in unqualified terms ("gave people/us rights"); those that qualified the definition ("some people got rights," or "didn't give black people rights"), and those that related to the criminal justice system ("you have rights if you're arrested"). Similarly, in coding explanations related to nation building actors and events, explanations tended to fall into patterns which construed national formation or development in positive terms ("Louisiana Purchase expanded the nation") or qualified or negative terms ("American Revolution gave people independence but black people were still slaves").

Besides nation building and individual rights, there were race-related differences in three other categories. One referred to how students depicted race relations historically. I examined how students depicted Native American-white and white-black relations. I examined whether they referred to whites as perpetrators ("whites caused racism against Indians"), allies ("white people helped blacks escape on the Underground Railroad), friends ("Pilgrims and Indians had dinner as friends") or absent from explanations related to racial oppression ("black people were slaves and they did the work"). I also coded explanations according to whether or the extent to which they depicted Native Americans and African Americans as historical subjects, as well as victims. The third code related to students' use of "identity" terms such as "I/me" or "we/us" when referring to actors and events. White students used them when discussing nation building actors ("George Washington was *our* first president") or events ("the American Revolution started *us* on the road to getting *our* own county"), while black students used them when explaining blacks' experiences ("Martin Luther King, Jr. stood up for *us*" or "Northern migration was when *my* family came North").

As I coded the explanations, I engaged in comparative analyses of explanations (LeCompte & Schensul, 1999). At the beginning of the year, I conducted comparative analyses within racial groups to assess similarities, differences and range of responses, and then between racial groups in assessing the same aspects of explanations. At the end of the year , I conducted comparative analyses within and between racial groups *across* time periods (comparing beginning- and end-of-the-year explanations) to assess the effects of instruction on students' understandings. I also began to focus on differences in white and black students' explanations. Rather than discuss similarities (i.e. most white and black eighth and eleventh graders selected the invention of the car and airplane because they "led to faster transportation"), I focused on differences because they had pedagogical implications for teaching history in public schools.

After I coded individual selections and explanations, I then grouped explanations of actors/events into chronological/periodic categories, such as national formation and early national history, Civil War period, World War II, etc. Within each category, I examined how students explained actors/events related to nation building, rights, African American experiences, and race relations, codes for which I found race-related differences. By grouping and categorizing explanations across time periods, as well as examining the themes of historical change and continuity that adolescents gave in response to the third part of the task, I constructed the interpretive frameworks or "webs of knowledge, beliefs, and associations" (Wertsch, 2002) students called upon to describe specific historical actors/events and interpret the "whole" or overarching themes of national history.

From the analyses, I found that white students generally constructed positive and progressive interpretations of national history, one in which Europeans and European Americans or whites discovered and/or founded a nation based on freedom and rights, blacks and women eventually fought for and achieved equal rights, and U.S. democracy expanded over time to include all Americans and expanded oversees to bring democracy abroad. They constructed and affiliated with a national identity based on concepts of freedom and individual rights and saw contemporary society in a positive light. Black students constructed much more tempered or pessimistic interpretations of U.S. history and society. They constructed the nation as having been founded by and for white people who enslaved and violated Africans and African Americans. Continual racism rather than expanding rights exemplified national development, and although the nation made progress in terms of rights, racism and other forms of inequality still marked contemporary society. Black students constructed a national identity based on racism and other forms of inequality and affiliated with a collective "black" identity, exemplified by the contributions and experiences of African Americans historically.

Similarities and Differences Across Grade Levels

Eleventh graders had the most sophisticated and elaborated explanations and were more likely than eighth graders to give more than one explanation for an actor's/event's significance. Eighth graders tended to give one explanation for actors/event, except for well known ones or ones in which the teacher spent a significant amount of instructional time. Fifth graders' explanations were the most simple, often limited to a few words or a phrase. I applied the coding system to the explanations of the eighth and eleventh graders. Fifth graders' explanations, however, were simple and straightforward and I simply tallied these. For example, in explaining Martin Luther King, Jr., fifth graders made statements like "helped blacks get rights" or "gave speeches" and I created codes "rights for blacks" or "gave speeches." Unlike eighth and eleventh graders, fifth graders had not constructed an interpretive framework of overarching sets of themes which characterized their views of U.S. history. Rather their knowledge and beliefs were more fragmentary and tied to individual historical actors or events. They did not seem to possess an interpretive framework which related concepts between or across specific actors or events (McKeown & Beck, 1990; VanSledright & Brophy, 1992).

References

Almarza, D. (2001). Contexts shaping minority language students' perceptions of American history. *Journal of Social Studies Research, 25,* 4–22.

Alridge, D. P. (2006). The limits of master narratives in history textbooks: An analysis of representations of Martin Luther King, Jr. *Teachers College Press, 108,* 662–686.

Anderson, J. D. (1994). How we learn race through history. In L. Kramer (Ed.). *Learning history in America: Schools, culture, and politics* (pp. 87–106). Minneapolis, MN: University of Minnesota Press.

Apple, M. W. & Buras, K. L. (2006). *The subaltern speak: Curriculum, power and educational struggles.* New York: Routledge.

Avery, P.G. & Hahn, C.L. (2004). Diversity and U.S. 14-year-olds' knowledge, attitudes, and experiences. In W. Stephan, & P. Vogt (Eds.). *Education programs for improving intergroup learning* (pp. 195–210). New York: Teachers College Press.

Ball, A. F. (2006). *Multicultural strategies for education and social change: Carriers of the torch in the United States and South Africa.* New York: Teachers College Press.

Banks, J. A. (1991). Multicultural education: Its effects on students' racial and gender role attitudes. In J. Shaver (Ed.). *Handbook of teaching and learning in social studies education.* New York: Macmillan.

Banks, J. A. (1997). *Educating citizens for a multicultural society.* New York: Teachers College Press.

Banks, J. A. (2004). Race, knowledge construction, and education in the USA: Lessons from history. *Race, Ethnicity, and Education, 5,* 7–27.

Barton, K. C. & Levstik, L. S. (1998). "It wasn't a good part of history": National identity and students' explanations of historical significance. *Teachers College Record, 99,* 478–513.

Barton, K. C. & Levstik, L. S. (2004). *Teaching history for the common good.* Mahwah: NJ: Lawrence Erlbaum Press.

Barton, K. C. & McCully, A. W. (2005). History, identity and the school curriculum in Northern Ireland: An empirical study of secondary students' ideas and perspectives. *Journal of Curriculum Studies, 37,* 85–116.

Bell, L. A. (2002). Sincere fictions: The pedagogical challenges of preparing white teachers for multicultural classrooms. *Equity and Excellence in Education, 35,* 236–244.

Bennet, W. J. (2003). *Why we fight: Moral clarity and war on terrorism.* New York: Regnery Publishing.

Bolgatz, J. (2005). *Talking race in the classroom.* New York: Teachers College Press.

Bonilla-Silva, E. (2003). *Racism without racists: Color-blind racism and the persistence of racial inequality in the United States.* Lanham, MD: Rowman & Littlefield.

Brophy, J. (1999). Elementary students learn about Native Americans: The development of empathy. *Social Education, 63,* 39–45.

Brown, C. S. (2002). *Refusing racism: White allies and the struggle for civil rights.* New York: Teachers College Press.

Bryant, A. (1992, February 25). Michigan workers see politics in closing. *New York Times,* C1, C3.

Chase, S. E. (2005). Narrative inquiry: Multiple lenses, approaches, voices. In N. K. Denzin & Y. S. Lincoln (Eds.). *The Sage handbook of qualitative research,* 3rd Ed. (pp. 651–680).

Cooks, J. & Epstein, T. (2000). Dissin' democracy? African American adolescents' concepts of citizenship. *Journal of Social Studies Research, 40,* 10–20.

Cornbleth, C. & Waugh, D. (1995). *The great speckled bird: Multicultural politics and education policymaking.* New York: St. Martin's Press.

Davis, O. L., E. A. Yeager, & S. J. Foster (Eds.) (2001). *Historical empathy and perspective taking in the social studies.* New York: Rowman & Littlefield Publishers.

Department of Education (1996). *Social studies curriculum framework.* Lansing, MI: Michigan Department of Education.

Derman-Sparks, L. & Phillips, C. B. (1997). *Teaching/learning anti-racism: A developmental approach.* New York: Teachers College Press.

Derman-Sparks, L. & Ramsey, P. (2003). *What if all the kids are white? Anti-bias multicultural education with young children and families.* New York: Teachers College Press.

DeSmit, K. (1992, July 8). Closing of Oakdale plant has employees living on edge. *Detroit News & Free Press,* 1, 13.

Dickar, M. (in press). Hearing the silenced dialogue: An examination of the impact of teacher race on their experiences.

Dickerson, M. (1992, February 25). Depression: First hurdle for targeted workers. *Detroit News,* 7A.

Dimitriadis, G. (2000). "Making history go" at a local community center: Popular media and the construction of historical knowledge among African American youth. *Theory and Research in Social Education, 28,* 40–64.

Dutro, E., Kazemi, E., & Balf, R. (2006). About your color, that's personal: A critical discourse analysis of race and resistance in an urban elementary classroom. Paper presented at the Annual Meeting of the American Educational Research Association.

Eisner, E. W. (1991). *The enlightened eye: Qualitative inquiry and the enhancement of educational practice.* Toronto: Macmillan Publishers.

Epstein, T. (1993). Multiculturalism and the politics of history: A response to Thomas Sobol. *Teachers College Record, 95*, 273–282.

Epstein, T. (1996). Urban adolescents' historical understanding: Differences in Black and White. *Theory and Research in Social Education, 26*, 399–402.

Epstein, T. (1997). Sociocultural approaches to young people's historical understanding. *Social Education, 61*, 28–31.

Epstein, T. (1998). Deconstructing differences in African-American and European- American adolescents' perspectives on U.S. history. *Curriculum Inquiry, 28*, 397–423.

Epstein, T. (2000). Adolescents' perspectives on racial diversity in United States history: Case studies from an urban classroom. *American Educational Research Journal, 37*, 185–214.

Epstein, T. (2001). Race, research and social education. *Theory into Practice, 40*, 42–47.

Epstein, T. (2002). History, pedagogy, and racial identity in an urban community. Presentation at the University of Colorado-Boulder School of Education.

Epstein, T. (2006). The effects of family/community and school discourses on children's and adolescents' interpretations of United States history. *International Journal of Historical Learning, Teaching and Research, 6*, 1–9.

Epstein, T. (2007a). *Teaching about race in urban history classrooms: The effects of culturally responsive teaching.* Spencer Foundation grant #20080060.

Epstein, T. (2007b). The role of social identities in the formation of historical interpretation. Paper presented at the History Educators International Research Network Conference in Istanbul, Turkey.

Epstein, T. & Shiller, J. (2005). Perspective matters: Social identity and the teaching and learning of national history. *Social Education, 69*, 201–204.

Evans, R. (2004). *The social studies wars: What should we teach the children?* New York: Teachers College Press.

Fine, M. (1993). "You can't just say that the only ones who can speak are those who agree with your position": Political discourse in the classroom. *Harvard Educational Review, 63*, 412–433.

Fine, M. (1995). *Habits of mind: Struggling over values in America's classrooms.* Hoboken, NJ: Jossey Bass.

Fogel, H. (1992, May 13). GM: Oakdale jobs were not guaranteed. *Detroit News*, 1E, 4E.

Fogel, H. (1993, March 31). Workers cling to hope as GM seeks fast ruling. *Detroit News*, 6.

Foner, E. (1999). *The story of American freedom.* New York: Norton Press.

Franklin, J. H. & Moss, A. A. (2000). *From slavery to freedom: A history of African Americans*, 8th Ed. New York: Knopf Publishing.

George, M. (1992, February 1). Oakdale area already sees a shrinkage. *Detroit News & Free Press*, 1A, 8A.

George. M. (1993, January 23). Township, GM told to settle dispute. *Detroit News & Free Press*, 1–2.

Grant, S. G. (2003). *History lessons: Teaching, learning, and testing in U.S. high school classrooms.* Mahwah, NJ: Lawrence Erlbaum Associates.

Grant, S. G. (2006). *Measuring history: Cases of state-level testing across the United States.* Charlotte, NC: Information Age Publishing.

Grosvenor, I. (2000). "History for the nation": Multiculturalism and the teaching of history (pp. 148–158). In J. Arthur & R. Phillips (Eds.). *Issues in History Teaching.* London: Routledge.

Gutierrez, C. (2000). Making connections: The interdisciplinary community of teaching and learning history. In P. Stearns, P., Seixas, & S. Wineburg (Eds.) *Knowing, teaching, and learning history: National and international perspectives.* New York: New York University Press.

Gutierrez, K., Rymes, B., & Larson, J. (1995). Script, counterscript, and underlife in the classroom. James Brown versus Brown v. Board of Education. *Harvard Educational Review, 65,* 445–472.

Gwaltney, J. L. (1993). *Drylongo: A self-portrait of black America.* New York: The New Press.

Harlan, C. & Mitchell, J. (1992, February 25). Rage, relief and warning to UAW mark GM decision on closing plant. *Wall Street Journal*, A8.

Hayes, T. C. (1991, December 19). Tug of war at G.M. plant closing. *Detroit News*, D1–4,5.

Hernandez, R. (1992a, February 25). There's a lot of broken dreams. *Detroit News*, 4A.

Hernandez, R. (1992b, March 6). Shutdown stress hits Willow Run, *The Detroit News*, 1B.

Hess, D. E. (2005). Moving beyond celebration: Challenging curricular orthodoxy in the teaching of Brown and its legacy. *Teachers College Record, 107,* 2046–2067.

Hess, D. & Posselt, J. (2002). How high school students experience and learn from the discussion of controversial public issues. *Journal of Curriculum and Supervision, 17,* 283–314.

Holt, T. (1995). Marking: Race, race making, and the writing of history. *American Historical Review, 100,* 1–20.

Horton, J. O. & Horton, L. E. (2001). *Hard road to freedom: The story of African American.* New Brunswick, NJ: Rutgers University Press.

Howard, T. C. (2004). "Does race really matter?" Secondary students' constructions of racial dialogue in the social studies. *Theory and Research in Social Education, 32,* 484–485.

Hursh, D. W. & Ross, E. W. (2000). *Democratic social education: Social studies for social change.* New York: Taylor & Francis Publishers.

Kaufman, D., Johnson, S. M., Kardos, S. M., Liu, E., & Peske, H. G. (2002). "Lost at sea": New teachers' experiences with curriculum and assessment. *Teachers College Record, 104,* 273–300.

Keyssar, A. (2000). *The right to vote: The contested history of democracy in the United States*. New York: Basic Books.

Kinder, D. R. & Sanders, L. M. (1997). *Divided by color: Racial politics and democratic ideals*. Chicago, IL: University of Chicago Press.

King, J. (1992). Diaspora literacy and consciousness in the struggle against miseducation in the black community, *Journal of Negro Education, 61*, 317–340.

Ladson-Billings, G. (1994). *The dreamkeepers*. San Francisco, CA: Jossey-Bass.

Ladson-Billings, G. (1995). *The dreamkeepers: Successful teachers of African American teachers*. San Francisco, CA: Jossey Bass Publishers.

Ladson-Billings, G. (Ed.) (2003). *Critical race theory perspectives on the social studies: The profession, policies, and curriculum*. Greenwich, CT: Information Age Publishing.

LeCompte, M. D. & Schensul, J. (1999). *Analyzing and interpreting ethnographic data*. Lanham, MD: Altamira Press.

Lee, C. D. (2006). "Every good-bye ain't gone": Analyzing the cultural underpinnings of classroom talk. *International Journal of Qualitative Studies in Education, 19*, 305–327.

Levin, D. (1991, December 19). General Motors to cut 70,000 jobs; 21 plants to shut. *New York Times*, A1; D4.

Levin, D. (1993, August 5). Court backs G.M. on plant closing. *New York Times*, 1, 8 F.

Levstik, L. S. (2000). Articulating the silences: Teachers' and adolescents' conceptions of historical significance. In P. Stearns, P. Seixas, & S. Wineburg (Eds.). *Knowing, teaching, and learning history: National and international perspectives* (pp. 284–305). New York: New York University Press.

Levstik, L. S. & Barton, K. C. (2005). *Doing history: Investigating with children in elementary and middle school*. Mahwah, NJ: Lawrence Erlbaum Press.

Lewis, A. E. (2003). *Race in the schoolyard: Negotiating the color line in classrooms and communities*. New Brunswick, NJ: Rutgers University Press.

Loewen, J. W. (1995). *Lies my teacher told me: Everything your American history textbook got wrong*. New York: New Press.

Marri, A. R. (2005). Building a framework for classroom-based multicultural democratic education: Learning from three skilled teachers. *Teachers College Record, 107*, 1036–1059.

McIntosh, P. (1990). *White privilege: Unpacking the invisible knapsack*. Working Paper 189. Wellesley, MA.: Wellesley College Center for Research on Women.

McIntyre, P. (1997). *Making meaning of whiteness: Exploring racial identity with white teachers*. Albany, NY: SUNY Press.

McKeown, M. G. & Beck, I. L. (1990). The assessment and characterization of young learners' knowledge of a topic in history. *American Educational Research Journal, 27*, 688–726.

McNeil, L. (1986). *Contradictions of control: School structure and school knowledge.* New York: Routledge Press.

Moreau, J. (2003). *Schoolbook nation: Conflicts over American history textbooks from the Civil War to the present.* Ann Arbor, MI: University of Michigan Press.

Nash, G., Crabtree, C., & Dunn, R. (2000). *History on trial: Culture wars and the teaching of the past.* New York: Vintage.

National Council for the Social Studies (1994). *Expectations of excellence: Curriculum standards for the social studies.* Silver Spring, MD: National Council for the Social Studies.

Naughton, K. (1993, August 5). GM closer to closing Oakdale, but township fights on. *Detroit News*, 1, 12–13A.

New York Department of Education (1996). *Learning standards in social studies.* Albany, NY: Department of Education.

Niemi, R. G. & Junn, J. (2005). *Civic education: What makes students learn.* New Haven, CT: Yale University Press.

Parker, W. C. (2003). *Teaching democracy: Unity and diversity in public life.* New York: Teachers College Press.

Parker, W. C. (2006). Public discourses in schools: Purposes, problems, possibilities. *Educational Researcher, 35*, 11–18.

Payne, C. M. (2003). More than a symbol of freedom: Education for liberation and democracy. *Phi Delta Kappan, 85*, 22–28.

Pollock, M. (2004). *Colormute: Race talk dilemmas in an American schools.* Princeton, NJ: Princeton University Press.

Ravitch, D. (1990). Multiculturalism: *E pluribus plures. American Scholar, 90*, 337–354.

Rimer, S. (1992, September 7). American dream put on hold at car plant doomed to shut. *New York Times*, 1, 40–41.

Rosenzweig, R. & Thelen, D. (1998). *The presence of the past: Popular uses of history in American life.* New York: Columbia University Press.

Rubin, B. (2007). "There's still no justice": Youth civic identity and development amid distinct school and community contexts. *Teachers College Record, 2*, 449–481.

Schlesinger, A. M, Jr. (1992). *The disuniting of America.* New York: Norton.

Schuman, H., Steeh, C, Bobo, L., & Krysan, M. (1997). *Racial attitudes in America: Trends and interpretations*, Rev. Ed. Cambridge, MA: Harvard University Press.

Schweber, S. A. (2004). *Making sense of the Holocaust: Lessons from classroom practice.* New York: Teachers College Press.

Schweber, S. (2006). Fundamentally 9/11: The fashioning of collective memory in a Christian school. *American Journal of Education,112*, pp. 392–417.

Schweber, S.A. & Irwin, R. (2003). "Especially special": Learning about Jews in a fundamentalist Christian school. *Teachers College Record, 105*, 1693–1719.

Sears, D. O., Sianius, J., & Bobo, L. (2000). *Racialized politics: The debate about racism in America*. Chicago, IL: University of Chicago Press.

Segall, A. (1999). Critical history: Implications for history/social studies education. *Theory and Research in Social Education, 27,* 358–374.

Segall, A. (2006). Teaching history in the age of accountability: Measuring history or measuring up to it? In S. G. Grant (Ed.). *Measuring history: Cases of state-level testing across the United States.* Charlotte, NC: Information Age Publishing.

Seixas, P. (1993). Historical understanding among adolescents in a multicultural setting. *Curriculum Inquiry, 23,* 281–304.

Seixas, P. (2000). Schweigen! Die Kinder! Or, Does postmodern history have a place in schools? In P. Stearns, P. Seixas, & S. Wineburg (Eds.). *Knowing, teaching, and learning history: National and international perspectives* (pp. 19–37). New York: New York University Press.

Shemilt, D. (1980). *Evaluation study: Schools council history 13–16 project.* Edinburgh: Holmes McDougall.

Shemilt. C. (2000). The Caliph's coin: The currency of narrative frameworks in history teaching. In P. Stearns, P. Seixas, & S. Wineburg, (Eds.). *Knowing, teaching, and learning history: National and international perspectives* (pp. 83–101). New York: New York University Press.

Sleeter, C. E. (2001). Preparing teachers for culturally diverse schools: Research and the overwhelming presence of whiteness. *Journal of Teacher Education, 52,* 94–106.

Sleeter, C. E. (2005). *Un-standardizing curriculum: Multicultural teaching in the standards based classroom.* New York: Teachers College Press.

Sleeter, C. E. & Stillman, J. (2005). Standardizing knowledge in a multicultural society. *Curriculum Inquiry, 35,* 27–36.

Smith, R. (1997). *Civic ideals: Conflicting visions of citizenship in U.S. history.* New Haven, CT: Yale University Press.

Stanley, W. B. (2001). *Critical issues in social studies research for the twenty-first century.* Greenwich, CT: Information Age Publishing.

Stearns, P., Seixas, P., & Wineburg, S. (Eds.) (2000). *Knowing, teaching, and learning history: National and international perspectives.* New York: New York University Press.

Sugrue, T. (1996). *The origins of the urban crisis: Race and inequality in postwar Detroit.* Princeton, NJ: Princeton University Press.

Symcox, L. (2002). *Whose history? The struggle for national standards in American classrooms.* New York: Teachers College Press.

Terkel, S. (2005). *Race: How Blacks and Whites think and feel about the American obsession.* New York: Random House.

Trainor, J. S. (2005). "My ancestors didn't own slaves": Understanding white talk about race. *Research in the teaching of English, 40,* 140–167.

U.S. Census Bureau (1990). *Statistical abstracts of the United States.* Washington, DC: Government Printing Office.

U.S. Census Bureau (2000). *Statistical abstracts of the United States.* Washington, DC: Government Printing Office.

Van Hover, S. (2006). Teaching history in the old dominion: The impact of Virginia's accountability reform on seven secondary beginning history teachers. In S. G. Grant (Ed.). *Measuring history: Cases of state-level testing across the United States.* Charlotte, NC: Information Age Publishing.

VanSledright, B. A. (1998). On the importance of historical positionality to thinking about and teaching history. *International Journal of Social Education, 12,* 1–18.

VanSledright, B. A. (2001). From empathic regard to self-understanding: Im/positionality, empathy and historical contextualization. In O. L. Davis, E. A. Yeager, & S. J. Foster (Eds.). *Historical empathy and perspective taking in the social studies.* New York: Rowman & Littlefield Publishers.

VanSledright, B. A. (2002). *In search of America's past: Learning to read history in elementary school.* New York: Teachers College Press.

VanSledright, B. & Brophy, J. (1992). Storytelling, imagination and fanciful elaboration in children's historical reconstructions. *American Educational Research Journal, 29,* 837–859.

Villegas, A. M. & Lucas, T. (2002). *Educating culturally relevant teachers: A coherent approach.* New York: SUNY Press.

Wertsch, J. V. (2000). Is it possible to teach beliefs, as well as knowledge about history? In P. Stearns, P. Seixas, & S. Wineburg (Eds.). *Knowing, teaching, and learning history* (pp. 38–50). New York: New York University Press.

Wertsch, J. V. (2002). *Voices of collective remembering.* New York: Cambridge University Press.

Wills, J. S. (1994). Popular culture, curriculum and historical representation: The situation of Native Americans in American history and the perpetuation of stereotypes. *Journal of Narrative and Life History, 4,* 277–294.

Wills, J. S. (1996). Who needs multicultural education?: White students, U.S. history and the construction of a usable past. *Anthropology and Education Quarterly, 27,* 365–389.

Wills, J. S., Lintz, A., & Mehan, H. (2004). Ethnographic studies of multicultural education in U.S. classrooms and schools. In J. A. Banks (Ed). *Handbook of Research on Multicultural Education,* 2nd Ed. New York: Macmillan.

Wineburg, S. (2000). *Historical thinking and other unnatural acts: Charting the future of teaching the past.* Philadelphia, PA: Temple University Press.

Wineburg, S., Mossborg, S., Porat, D., & Duncan, A. (2007). Common belief and the cultural curriculum: An intergenerational study of historical consciousness. *American Educational Research Journal, 44,* 40–76.

Wynter, S. (1992). *Do not call us Negroes: How multicultural textbooks perpetuate racism.* San Jose, CA: Aspire Books.

Yeager, E. A. & Terzian, S. G. (2007). "That's when we became a nation": Urban Latino adolescents and the designation of historical significance. *Urban Education, 42,* 52–81.

Zimmerman, J. (2002). *Whose America? Culture wars in the public schools.* Cambridge, MA: Harvard University Press.

Index

Note: Roman numbers are for pages in the Preface at the front of the book, e.g. social justice xv–xvi, xix, 3, 4–5, 59, 117–19

Page numbers followed by 'n' are for footnotes, e.g. African Americans 27n1, 109–10

violence: black-on-black 107, 109; and lessons of history 94–5; race relations as 46–50; racial 68, 74–5, 82–3

voting rights: teachers' pedagogy on 38–9, 45

wars: black participation in 17–18, 66, 80, 97; black participation in American Revolution 122; black participation in Civil War 23, 58; black participation in Vietnam 101; and role of nation in history 69, 94–5; role of, in national history 63–4, 76, 77, 91, 92

Washington, George 16, 66

websites 126–7, 128, 133, 136

Wertsch, J.V. xv, 13, 145

West, C.: *Race Matters* 131

westward migration 50–1, 62

white parents: and history at home 94–6; interpretive frames for history and society 11, 89–92, 102, 112–13; views on citizenship 92–4; views on school history 92–4

white racism *see* racism

white students: on civic responsibility 106; and classroom discussion 6, 129–30, 132; compared with black 71, 86–8; effects of pedagogies on 10, 71–2, 86–8, 123, 133–4; interpretive frames for history and society xx–xxi, 1–2, 3, 10, 61–5, 72–80, 145; on national development and identity 16, 63–4, 75–6, 77, 112–13; on overall historical themes 11–12, 64–5, 76–80; on race relations 62–3, 74–5; on racial groups 61–2, 72–4;

research analysis for 142, *see also* adolescents; black students; interpretive frames

white teachers: and "race talk" 9–10, 118–19

white-Native American relations: black parents views on 96; black students' views on 67, 82; in curricular standards 125; teachers' pedagogies on 41–2, 47, 50–1, 53; white parents' views on 90–1; white students' views on 74, *see also* European American history

whites: black adolescents' views on 107, 108; black parents' views on 98, 101; and Civil Rights Movement 45; and constitutional rights 37–8; and enslavement 43, 57–8, 131–2; as racial group 32–5, 131; support for black freedom movements 122–3; use of term 'white' 27n1; white adolescents' views on 65, 79; white parents' views on 91, 93, 95, *see also* European American history; white-Native American relations

Wills, J.S. xv, 10, 116; Lintz, A., and Mehan, H. 10

Wineburg, S. xvii, 5, 13, 14

women: discrimination against black 86; employment of 23, 45; suffrage 77, 92–3

World War II: parents' views on 91, 96; students' views on 63, 66, 69, 76, 77, 80; teachers' presentations of 16, 18–19, 27, 76, 80

Wounded Knee, Battle of 51

writing practises 130